Reconstructing Reality

Book II of
Visions from Venus

a novel by

Suzanne Lie, Ph.D.

PREFACE

Dear Reader,

Since you have been attracted to this book, you are likely to be one of the many who has volunteered to enter into the processes of remembering your multidimensional heritage and uniting with your true SELF. Achieving this unity would be difficult indeed with the knowledge of only one lifetime. Fortunately, once you have healed "enough" of your present reality (life) so that your higher vision is restored, your other realities (lives) clamor to the surface of your consciousness to be healed, as well.

Reconstructing Reality is a journey to the Violet Temple of Transmutation on fifth dimensional Venus. From this fifth dimensional perspective, it is possible to release your lives-long belief in the illusion of separation and limitation so that you can view your many lives on third and fourth dimensional Earth. From the Violet Temple, you can assist whichever lifetime is in need of transmuting the fears of that reality into love. In that way, you can recover the wisdom that was hidden within the pain of that life and illuminate your present reality.

Most of you in the third dimension do not remember that you have volunteered to take on your current life. However, as each of you begins to awaken to your true Selves, you remember your life "in between" death and birth, other third dimensional realities, and lives on the higher dimensions. These other realities are actually occurring all at the same moment in different space-time coordinates. With the assistance of your fifth dimensional self, also known as your Soul, you can act as a "Higher Self" to these other third and fourth dimensional realities.

The fourth dimension is known as the Astral Plane. It is the plane of reality one octave above the third dimensional, physical world. The fourth dimension is the realm of dreams, imagination, psychic ability, intuition, and creativity. The Gateway to the fourth dimension is opened through your unconscious and super conscious minds. Shamans, medicine men and women, true spiritual leaders and artists have been accessing the powers of the fourth dimension and using them in the third dimension since the beginning of "time."

The fifth dimension is a spiritual plane and is one octave above the fourth. It is a dimension beyond polarity, separation, limitation, matter, and time or space. Therefore, your fifth dimensional bodies are androgynous, simultaneously male and female, and made of Light. Some have called it the Soul Plane or Heaven. On this plane of existence, all inhabitants live in the Unity of the Oneness and the Hereness of the ever-present NOW.

Once you can be consciously aware of the higher dimensions while in your mundane, third dimensional reality, you can begin to bring that awareness into your everyday life. However, first you must do your homework. The higher dimensions are only open to you if you are willing to put aside your "time" in pursuit of these higher worlds. Exploration of the fourth dimension, however, is not always an enjoyable experience because the fourth dimension holds the sum total of all of your emotions and thoughts from all of your third and fourth dimensional lives.

Just as the murky water in a pond stays at the bottom and the clear, fresh water floats on the top; your unpleasant and painful memories lie on the floor of the fourth dimension—just beyond your third dimensional awareness. In order to cross the threshold into the higher worlds, you must be willing to face your history and clear a path through your accumulated fear and confusion. Then you can gain conscious access to your true multidimensional heritage.

All of you who have volunteered for this process of Awakening will have many initiations. These initiations are necessary to clear fear from your aura so that you can center your consciousness in Love. It is through the clearing of your aura, and therefore the aura of Mother Earth upon whom you live, that you will assist in the healing and ascension of the planet. When you view each of your "past lives," you can assist these portions of your Self with the initiations of that life time. You can commune with them at the moment of decision within their initiation so that a resolution, which was not there before, can be accomplished.

When you remember your fifth dimensional SELF in the fifth dimension, you will have a direct view of the many lives that are being played out in the time and space of the physical world. In the fifth dimension, there is no time or space. Therefore, you can view each alternate reality— no matter where, no matter when. As you view the important moments of decision in each life, you can guide that "self" to make these decisions from love and not from fear. At this junction of decision-making, the reality you are healing will split into reality/parallel-reality with one reality following fear and the other reality following love. Your "fear reality" will exist as a lesson; however, your Soul's consciousness will be able to experience the "love reality" as well.

Once fear can be transformed into love in other realities, where it is easier to be objective, that transformation can more easily happen in your present reality. While you are learning this process of transmutation, it is best to move calmly and slowly throughout your day. In this way, you can keep your consciousness clear and receptive to your higher guidance. This guidance will assist you in grounding into your present, physical self (life) the lessons that you have learned from your other selves (lives), thereby making it easier to see the ramifications of every action and reaction that you choose.

When you are falling into the mire of the third dimension, call on your higher guidance, and it will throw you a lifeline. As your consciousness expands beyond the boundaries of your present physical self, you are freed from the limitations of the illusion of time. Just as you are the "future self" of your "past lives," your higher guidance is the "future self" of your "present self." Any corrections made in past lives are brought forward to your present reality and to your future self. Just as the computer adjusts the document when new information is input into a written paragraph, there are adjustments brought into future realities as you make changes in past or present ones.

Since time is actually radial, instead of linear, improvements made in any reality send a ripple of positive energy through all the other realities. Because of this ripple, healing a few focal lives can heal many other lives as well. Unfortunately, the law is true in the reverse, and any damage done to a few focal lives will also send a ripple of negativity through all your other lives. Therefore, be careful. Any choice of action, or reaction, has ramifications far beyond what is apparent within that particular host life.

Your challenges are great, but the process of Awakening is joyous beyond your imagination. Allow your SELF to assist you in fulfilling the Mission for which you volunteered and to remember your higher consciousness.

For more information about this process,
please see my website:
www.multidimensions.com

Enjoy Your Journey
Suzanne Lie

Copyright ® Suzanne Lie, Ph.D.

We invite you to respect the intellectual property of the author, and know that this e-book shall not be reproduced or shared by any electronic or mechanical means, including, but not limited to printing, file sharing, and email.

This e-book is licensed for your personal enjoyment, and if you enjoy it so and wish to share this book with another person, we encourage you to purchase an additional copy for each person individually. Thank you for respecting the hard work of this author.

Enjoy the story!

www.multidimensions.com

Published by

Multidimensional Press

Part One

The Violet Temple

VENUS

HOME
Chapter One

INNOCENCE
Chapter Two

COURAGE
Chapter Three

GUILT

UNWORTHINESS
Chapter Four

ABANDONMENT
Chapter Five

RELEASING THE VICTIM
Chapter Six

Part Two

Initiations
I AM

THE VORTEX
Chapter Seven

THE PRIEST
Chapter Eight

THE MEDICINE MAN
Chapter Nine

THE INNER GODDESS

THE PRIESTESS OF DELPHI
Chapter Ten

IN SERVICE TO THE GODDESS
Chapter Eleven

LIFE AFTER BIRTH
Chapter Twelve

EPILOGUE

RECOGNITION OF COMPLETION

Cast of Characters

Part One
The Violet Temple

The Guide - Shature's mentor on Venus
Lamire - Shature's Divine Complement
Lamira – Shature's fifth dimensional Venusian name
Lamerius – Androgynous name of Lamire and Lamira as ONE
Francesca - Shature's female incarnation in 13th century Italy
Illiana - Shature's female incarnation during World War II
The Gambler - Shature's male incarnation in 19th century England
The Deserter - Shature's male incarnation in 19th Century America
Nubnoset - Shature's female incarnation in ancient Egypt
Nephrite - Nubnoset's daughter

Part Two
INITIATIONS

Rahotep - Shature's male incarnation as an Initiate in ancient Egypt
How-ta-shai - Shature's incarnation as a Native American Medicine Man
Matia - Shature's incarnation as a Priestess of Delphi in ancient Greece
Mikeal - Matia's husband
Zulia - Matia's friend

PART 1
THE VIOLET TEMPLE

PROLOGUE

Shature awakened to total darkness. But had she been asleep? It had all seemed so real. Where had she been and where was she now? She attempted to sit up but found that she was in a small, enclosed space and appeared to be on a flat reclining chair. As she groped in the darkness above and around her, she discovered that she was enclosed in some kind of dome structure. Her mind tried to think ahead to plan a way out of the dome, but she was, instead, flooded by the memories of where she had been. No -- memories of WHOM she had been.

She had been a Priestess on Atlantis at the time of its final destruction. As the continent sank, Shature had had to hold her fear at bay while she experienced the ocean engulfing her. Suddenly, however, a bridge of light had released her consciousness from her dying physical form. The bridge, which joined Spirit and Matter, was created by the joint efforts of the physical ones and their Divine Complements in the fifth dimension. As she crossed the bridge, feelings of peace and joy replaced her fear. She saw Lamire, her Complement, standing before her with open arms and love in his eyes. Shature reached for him, but he was pulled away. A feeling of abandonment enveloped her.

Where was she now? The scene had changed. She was in spirit form trying to enter the body of a small child. She knew that she was part of a group of volunteers who had come from fifth dimensional Venus in response to third dimensional Earth's call for assistance. Her spirit was androgynous, male and female, but part of her, the male part, could not enter the child's body. On Venus, they had been androgynous, but on Earth the child's physical form could only hold the female portion of their essence. How could she exist as only half of a being? Shature pushed against the dome to find a way out. She felt as trapped by it as she had felt in her third dimensional skin. The vision changed.

The child was sitting on the edge of a cliff, curled up into a tiny ball and gazing off into the distant sky. Her heart was filled with such deep sorrow and suppressed rage at her abandonment that she could hardly breathe. The scenes blended into one, and Shature understood that the child was the one who would become the Priestess in Atlantis. Although Shature could not remember how she had come to be in this darkened dome or make sense of the many images that were like afterthoughts, she knew that she was neither the child nor the Priestess. She was not in Atlantis. But who was she, and where was she?

Suddenly, an image of the bright green fields of fourth dimensional Faerie filled her mind. A myriad number of flowers were in bloom, and the small flying creatures known as the Changers flitted about her head near a beautiful, violet flower that adorned her hair. The Changers' small sparkling auras blended with her own. Pleasure and contentment filled Shature's heart and she ceased pushing on the walls of the dome. She saw Lamire, her Divine Complement, walking beside her. They were in two bodies, but their hearts and minds were united in love and understanding. She relaxed into the image and reached to slip her arm through his, but as she did this, he disappeared.

All that was left was the darkness. Again the dome closed in on her. She felt a sense of urgency. She must find Lamire. He needed her, and he didn't even know it. She had lost him again, and he had lost himself. When would it end? She longed to be complete, male and female together in one form, androgynous like she had always been on…on where? She had known just a moment ago, but each image so engulfed her that she lost all sense of what she had experienced before.

A quickening in her womb distracted her thoughts. She was giving birth. This must also be an illusion, but her body felt each birth pain. Then she saw Lamire. His face was different, but the "feel" of him was the same. Somehow she knew that he was her husband, and they were on third dimensional Earth. They were in a large room that looked like a castle. The windows were mere slits, and tapestries hung on the stone walls in a futile attempt to keep out the damp cold. But Lamire's love warmed her through, as did the warmth of the newborn child. Her heart filled with a kind of love and contentment that could only be found in a physical form. She pulled the infant up to her breast to suckle and the scene changed as if in a dream.

Shature was floating above the same bed, but the form below her was now an old woman. It was she, and she was lying in her deathbed. The child she had birthed was now a mother and stood with the many crying loved ones gathered around the dying matriarch. Shature watched the scene from above. She wanted to tell them that she was fine, but she could not control the body below her. Peace and calm filled her as she floated out of the room. She felt a gentle touch and turned to find Lamire. His face was the one she had always known and his form was as ethereal as her own. He had come to take her Home. She reached for him, and the image faded.

All was total darkness again.

"Shature."

It was not Lamire's voice, yet it was familiar and seemed to be coming from below the dome while it also echoed in her mind.

"Shature, remember who you are."

Shature's chair lowered her out of the dome. The gentle voice of her Guide had restored her memory. A million conflicting emotions tried to find a place in her heart while her mind raced to understand all that she had experienced. As the chair settled to the floor of the circular room, she saw the kind face of her Guide.

"Do you see now why we waited so long before you revisited your first Earthly incarnations?" The Guide spoke in his usual telepathic manner.

"Y....Yes, I do," she stammered. "I am back on Venus, am I not?" Shature took a deep breath to try to center her self.

"Yes, my One, you are back on fifth dimensional Venus. You are between incarnations, studying your third dimensional lives on Earth." The Guide reached over and touched her shoulder. "The extreme emotions of your first Earthly experience pulled you from the awareness of your true self. Would you like to rest for a while?"

Shature nodded as she put her hand to her head.

"Perhaps a rest would help me regain my balance," she thought, remembering that all communication on Venus was telepathic.

"I suggest you merge with Lamire. I think that will bring you back to your Self."

Shature nodded again and sat up as she swung her legs to the floor. She felt dizzy and stood up slowly. Her Guide helped her to her feet and assisted her to the door. He was actually androgynous, but his main emanation was masculine. Leaning against his warm essence calmed and reassured Shature.

Thank you," she said as she left the room. "I know that if I merge back into Lamerius I will regain my strength."

Lamerius was the name of her complete, androgynous form. When she and Lamire studied with their individual guides in the Violet Temple at the threshold of fifth dimensional Venus, they separated into their male and female essence. She used the name Shature, rather than her Venusian name, Lamira, because it helped her identify with her Earth experiences. Often, in between their studies, they would rejoin into one being. Her Guide had told her that she was preparing for her final visit to third dimensional Earth. The wheel of the Great Cycle was closing, and the Venusians were being called back Home. It was important that before their final incarnation, they understood and balanced their Earthly lives from the fifth dimensional perspective of Venus.

CHAPTER ONE

HOME

Lamerius lay upon the warm pink sand of its special cove beneath the cliffs of Red Mountain. The Waters of Light gently caressed its feet and grounded its soul while the warm sand penetrated its aura. The Sun was descending towards the horizon, and it would soon be time to return to Temple studies. Lamerius was remembering its many third dimensional lives when it was separated into two different beings, masculine and feminine. Now it was once again one, androgynous body of Light. The re-joining of male and female into the ONE had enriched and healed both aspects of its essence. The male, Lamire, and the female, Lamira, communed what they had learned while apart. This communion brought much wisdom, clarity, peace, and most of all, unity.

Lamerius enjoyed the "no time" of fifth dimensional Venus where personal readiness created environmental markers to indicate that it was time to make a transition. When Lamerius was ready to return from its cycle of deep meditation, known on Earth as sleep, the Sun would rise. Then, when it was ready to take in the beautiful and healing love rays of the Venusian ecosystem, the Sun was high in the sky. Finally, when Lamerius was ready to separate into Lamire and Lamira and return to the Temple, the Sun was low upon the horizon.

On fifth dimensional Venus, there was no time-space continuum like there was on third dimensional Earth. Here, the environment was created, or rather chosen, by each member of the group consciousness. Each consensus reality was selected -- much like one would select a radio station or turn a page in a book. All the stations and pages existed simultaneously at all times, and one could choose what they desired to experience. Others who made the same choice also shared that reality.

Lamire and Lamira joined into Lamerius to share the experiences they had had while separated into two individual people. During their joining, Lamira related that "she" had just returned from reliving her first incarnation on third dimensional Earth. "I remember it all clearly now," she thought inside the Spirit of

Lamerius. "We chose to answer the call that Lady Gaia, Earth's consciousness, had put out at the end of the Atlanian era. Earth was on the verge of total destruction, because the balance of Light/Construction and Dark/Destruction was weighted toward the polarity of Destruction."

Lamerius remembered how it had studied here in fifth dimensional Venus in preparation for its adventure on Earth. Most of all, it remembered the shock of its first separation into its two polarized male and female individuals. Lamerius shuddered to remember how Lamira felt to be in a third dimensional body without her complete Self, and for Lamire to be without his feminine counterpart. It took many Earth years before Lamire and Lamira could accept their deep grief over living as only a portion of their total Self. It was in that first moment of separation that Lamerius first experienced the many limitations of third dimensional life.

Lamire and Lamira both carried those limitations, and the feelings of abandonment, through life after life after life. In spite of this, now both were soon to enter physical bodies again. Their commitment to Earth was ending, and they were free to return Home to Venus once and for all. First, however, each had to balance and heal the limited thoughts and painful emotions of their many earthly incarnations. This was best done at the source -- third dimensional Earth. Unfortunately, the strong, earthly illusions of limitation and separation clouded their memory of the parallel life that they also lived -- as an androgynous being on fifth dimensional Venus.

Lamerius stretched its Lightbody and a million sparkles fell upon the pink sand. Lamerius could feel the consciousness within every grain of sand and every pebble. It felt the aliveness of the air around it and the intelligent life force that cycled through its light body with every breath. The Waters of Light that caressed its feet grounded Lamerius into the matrix of this fifth dimensional hologram. Lamerius was fully aware that all matter and substance was an elaborate illusion created for the opportunity to commune and communicate with All That Is. Because the fifth dimension was a "half-way house" between the worlds of form and the worlds of formlessness, the holograms created there were often based on the forms and structures of the lower worlds.

Lamerius' light body was usually in the same humanoid form that its Divine Complements,

Lamire and Lamira, took while on Earth. However, it was not bound to that form. It was at liberty to alter its body in any way that it desired. If it wished to experience flying, it could grow the wings of an eagle, or become a bee. It could also float to its destination, as there was no gravity in the fifth dimension. When Lamerius traveled inter-dimensionally to the higher worlds it would often take on the form of a speck of light or a star being.

Lamerius' "skin" was translucent and glimmered with light, but it could look denser if it preferred. It was about ten Earth feet tall and, since it was composed of light, had no weight at all. Lamerius lived in the ever present NOW and was always in the Hereness and Isness of that Infinite Moment. When it separated into masculine and feminine to study in the Violet Temple, Lamerius still existed, but it "phased out" into the higher frequency of the fifth dimension until its two polarities, Lamire and Lamira, united again. It was the rejoining into one form that brought its light body into a slightly lower vibration. However, it never ceased to BE, as it was infinite and immortal.

If one of the Complements was "awake" in the lower worlds, Lamerius could send a stream of consciousness down the vibration scale and into his or her mind. Lamire and Lamira could also communicate with each other across all time and space through the "homing beam" of Lamerius' consciousness.

The Waters of Light had cooled and the sun hugged the horizon. It was "time" for Lamerius to separate again so that "The Two" could resume their individual Temple studies. Lamerius stood and stretched its long arms toward the top of Red Mountain. Its glowing, golden form expanded slowly, growing wider and wider until it took on the form of two pyramids attached at their base, with the masculine peak reaching towards the sky and the feminine peak grounded towards the heart of Venus. As the upper peak opened, the double pyramid slowly separated into two spirals of light. The spirals looked like spinning golden vortexes. Gradually, they unwound into two golden stars. Slowly, arms, legs and a head formed from the stars, and two separate beings emerged. Lamire and Lamira lifted their hands to the level of their hearts and touched each other, palm to palm.

"We will NOW return to the Temple," they spoke as they looked into each other's eyes. With a quick kiss and a smile, Lamira turned to take her separate path, but Lamire caught her by the arm.

"It is said that some of us will remain on Earth and assist in creating its new fifth dimensional reality. What do you think we will do?"

"I don't think that we can make that decision until we have finished our healing. After viewing our first separation, I realized the deep emotions of abandonment that were created. I am still clearing them from my third and fourth dimensional bodies."

"Yes, emotions are a constant challenge while in the astral and physical worlds. When we have learned to call on love to ease our fear, we will balance the polarities of the third and fourth dimension. Once the polarities are balanced, all judgments of 'good' or 'evil' can be released and mistakes can become lessons. Earth offers a great opportunity for that experience," chuckled Lamire.

"Yes, and that opportunity continues. I realized in my studies today that I have held resentment against you, against myself, since that first Atlantian embodiment. I felt abandoned, alone and angry when you could not join me in the physical body. I learned in my Temple studies that life after life I repeated that initial pattern of abandonment. I was afraid to trust, afraid to love, and all that I had left was hidden anger. Can you forgive me? Can I forgive myself?"

"I, too, created patterns that have been repeated," spoke Lamire. "After I was unable to enter the body with you I tried for days and months of your Earth time to contact you, but you could not hear me. If I lowered my vibration to the lower fourth dimension, my fear and sadness of losing you beckoned all the dark forces that were active around the planet at that time. Therefore, I had to call on you in your night body while you slept. We connected many times in that manner, but you were in such emotional turmoil that you forgot your dreams once you awakened. Before we had entered the third dimension, emotions of this kind were unknown. Therefore, when you first experienced them, you could not control them.

"Finally, when you were safe in the Atlantian Violet Temple, I was called back to Venus. There were many of us here who had not been able to enter the body with our other half. We banded together to form a group to guide our Divine Complements on Earth. Although I had not yet had a true physical experience, I felt yours, as we are truly one body. I felt all your anger, fear and sadness. Just as you felt as though you were only part of yourself, so did I. Those of us who had lost our Complements were different from the others.

"Although there is no judgment on Venus, I did not feel 'right' for a very long time. I was filled with an uncomfortable feeling of remorse. I had told you that I would lead, but you took charge and rushed in. Just as you carried a deep sense of abandonment, I carried a deep sense of guilt. I realize that part of the reason that I had difficulty communicating this to you is because of my guilt. In all of my Earth lives, whenever I met with a situation of abandonment, I responded with an ancient memory of guilt and shame. Perhaps, I also need to forgive both of us and the third dimension which caused us to be separated."

Lamire and Lamira were still after their confessions and apologies. Even though they knew what was in each other's heart and mind, the open communication was an important part of their healing. They both realized that it was their perception of separation from each other while in the third dimension that was their primary wound, but the separation was only an illusion. They were One with each other and with All That Is.

Could they remember that when they were back on Earth?

"The Sun is low," they said in one voice. "It is now our 'time' to return to our individual Temple studies. We will each ask our guides for assistance."

CHAPTER TWO

INNOCENCE

"Shature, I have felt your approach. Are you ready to resume your studies?" spoke the Guide as Shature entered the Temple.

"Yes, my Guide, I am. I feel different somehow. I feel as though I am on the verge of a great transition. I have merged with Lamire, and we have realized some patterns that we must heal. I know that I must heal my pattern of feeling abandoned, followed by my inability to trust, and an anger at the one that I felt abandoned by."

"Wonderful, my one, I have telepathically received your desire to view the lives in which you met Lamire and the various ways in which you danced the pattern of abandonment with your Divine Complement. Your desire will activate different third dimensional realities and program them into the dome. The dome will then present a holographic display of one time period at a time. You are actually entering that time frame, and any interaction that you have with its occupants is real and will most assuredly alter their reality.

"You will enter each life at a time when your third dimensional self will soon have to make an important life altering decision. Remember, even though you represent the female polarity and Lamire represents the male polarity, each of you has taken both male and female lives in your many journeys to third dimensional Earth.

When you make contact, you can assist each other in making his or her transitional decision based on love rather than fear. The choice of love over fear is what will heal your old wounds of abandonment. The vibration of love will remind you that you are never alone and that separation is only an illusion. Love will open the wounded heart to the unity and assistance of the higher worlds. Once the heart is open, it can be healed.

"Remember now," continued the Guide, "From this dimension, you can view your other realities anywhere along the space-time continuum, because in the fifth dimension we live in the omni-presence of the One. In this eternal now, time is perceived as a constant continuum that can be looked at as if it were spread out upon a table. Upon this table is a large circle that represents the time-space matrix of the third dimension. This large circle is made up of many small circles joined together, and each of these small circles represents a different third dimensional reality.

"From the perspective of third dimensional Earth, where the inhabitants are locked into the time-space matrix, they are not able to observe the nature of time from outside their experience of it. They measure the passage of time with calendars and clocks and have the experience of a past, a present, and a future. They are usually unaware of other third dimensional realities and, in fact, have a difficult enough time staying aware and fully conscious of the reality in which they are currently living.

"From the fourth dimension, the view of the time-space matrix is more objective. Time there is more fluid and mutable, but it does progress sequentially as in the third dimension. From the fourth dimension, one may even be able to observe, or interact with, inhabitants of different third dimensional realities. However, the vision is still very subjective, because the fourth dimension is plummeted by the backwash of the many thoughts and emotions of Earth inhabitants.

"In the fifth dimension, time does not pass, but you can pass into time. From here in the fifth dimension you can see that all time actually exists simultaneously. You can join with your third and fourth dimensional realities by viewing the holographic image that is displayed in the dome and merging your consciousness with this image. While viewing a hologram, you can observe an appropriate entry point. But remember, even though you may enter into any portion of Earth's time-space matrix, once you are there, you are bound by the progression of time as it is known on the third dimension.

"Yes, I understand," said Shature.

"Now, if you are ready, we will begin."

"Yes, I am ready. My joining with Lamire has completely refreshed me."

The Guide nodded and they floated together into the circular room that Shature had been using for her studies. She relaxed into the large reclining chair, which was positioned in the exact center of the room. The chair, which had now taken on much of her life essence, instantly conformed to fit her Lightbody and placed her in a prone position. As she rose into the domed ceiling above her, she merged with the holographic scene displayed there. The challenge was to maintain her objectivity as she observed, and sometimes experienced, her third dimensional life. The strong emotions of the physical plane often threatened to pull her into that reality. It was vital that she remember to maintain her fifth dimensional consciousness during any interactions with her physical embodiments so that she could serve as a Higher Self to guide them.

Shature focused on the scene before her and saw a young gypsy maiden in what seemed to be early Italy. She was lovely and had long black hair that touched her small waist. Her skin was light brown, and her eyes were as black as night. She had just unbraided her hair and was brushing it across her newly budding bosom.

"Tonight will be the night," murmured the maiden as she brushed her hair.

Shature could feel the maiden's physical vitality and emerging sexuality. She was definitely in the transition between childhood and womanhood. As Shature felt herself being drawn into that life, her observer self wondered if she would be able to reach that young, hopeful, and very naive maiden. And, if she did, could Shature maintain objectivity in the midst of such youth and passion?

* * *

Italy circa 1300

The night was clear, and the stars shone like a million candles in the distant sky. Through the flickering flames of the fire, Francesca could see the movement of his full green shirtsleeves as he played the guitar. The night was warm, and a gentle breeze caressed her face and played with her long, thick hair. The members of her camp, known as the Family, were around her. She felt their eyes upon her.

The warm breeze fanned the hot fire, which awakened a new sensuality in Francesca and inspired her to dance. As she whirled and moved, she felt his eyes upon her as he strummed his guitar. Francesca knew that she was a good dancer and that she could gain his recognition and approval. Perhaps now she was old enough. Always, in his eyes, she had been a child. Now, with her dance, she could prove to him that she had become a woman.

On and on she danced, with no fatigue, only exhilaration. She could feel herself going into a trance, but she did not try to stop it. She knew that with her trances came a freedom from limitation that she could never experience in her normal life. Although she had entered this state many times before, she usually remembered her experiences through a fog, as if it were a dream. This time she would stay conscious. She would go into her dream, only awake. She had waited many years for this night, and she vowed she would remember every moment of it.

Yes, he saw her. Tonight would be her turn. She was sure of it. From the corner of her eyes, Francesca saw that look of his that he saved for women he would lay with and horses that he would heal. He was renowned all over the countryside for the way he could gentle or heal the wildest or sickest horse. He was given much gold by the man of the house, and he was often paid by the woman of the house in the way in which women have been paying men for many eons.

Francesca knew, of course, that he had been with many women, but she didn't care. It only meant that his expertise could help her during her first experience. Francesca decided that she would make the first move. She began to dance slowly away from the fire and gradually into the darkness of the surrounding forest. After awhile she heard the music stop, and she knew it was because he had decided to follow her.

She hid behind the giant oak. This tree was special. She had sat many hours embraced by its roots. Whenever the gypsy family made their yearly stop in this valley, she would run to this tree like an old friend. She had even named him Octavos because, of course, it was male. Actually, she hadn't really named him; rather, the tree had told her his name.

But, enough of trees, tonight she was a woman, not a child. She had just finished her first moon blood, and now she could find out about that feeling that went with all the wonderful noises, and the reason for all that fighting.

She was so deep in her thoughts that she almost did not hear his approach. She "felt" him more than she heard him. And it wasn't in her heart that she felt him, but rather lower, in the crown of her budding womanhood.

The next morning came too soon. That evening, and in fact all through the night, was all she had hoped for. He had ignited a passion in her that she had never known. Francesca felt as though, she were the only one for him, even though she knew this could never be. He wasn't for just one woman. His life was one of conquest after conquest. Last night, however, she had been the conqueror and the conquered.

Night after night, she met him under the tree, and day after day she thought only of him. She could hardly do her chores because her mind was never on what she was doing. She thought always, and only, of him. But something was wrong. It had been several months and there had been no more moon-bloods, and now she felt ill every morning. Was she not a woman after all? Had she done this too soon? If she had, it would be breaking a very powerful taboo. A child was never supposed to know the love of a man, at least not in that way.

Francesca became more and more worried until finally she found she no longer enjoyed her long nights under the oak tree. Her breasts were sore when he touched them, and being with him was not as joyous a feeling as before. She no longer cared to sleep all night on the cold forest floor because she was sick in the morning. It seemed as if she were becoming less interested in his lovemaking. Eventually, he noticed her behavior and asked her what was wrong. After much denial of the problem, she finally told him of her fears and her illness. To her surprise, he laughed joyously and hugged her warmly.

"Why, Lovely (he always called her that), you are creating a son for me!" She was shocked. For all of her womanhood, how could she be so naive? Perhaps having a woman's body did not mean she had a woman's mind. She was sure that he would never marry her. He would never marry anyone. And as much as he was a marvelous lover, he would most assuredly be an awful husband. She had seen how tender and caring lovers had turned into cold and brutish husbands.

NO--she had no wish to marry him, but what of the baby? Why had she not thought of this before? This was more of the child's mind in the woman's body. Maybe she should run away. There seemed to be no other alternative. If she returned to her family, they would make her take the potion that ended these things, like they had done to her sister, or they would make her marry. NO--she would not marry. She would not be a gypsy wife like the other women in her camp, like her mother-- at least, not yet. But how could she kill this love child? Almost as soon as Francesca realized that she was with child, she began to love it. It was as if the love she had had for the man was somehow transferred to the child.

While all these thoughts rushed through her head, she heard him talking. He was saying that he would never neglect her. He was saying that he would love her even when she was old and fat and that they would have twelve children. What was he saying? He would never marry, she didn't want to be old and fat, and she certainly did NOT want twelve children. She wanted to be young and beautiful. She wanted to have fun, to taste life and to taste many lovers. She did not want to marry the first man she had been with. She wanted to experience the variety and diversity that she had seen the men enjoy.

She needed time to think. She needed to be away from him and away from her family. But how? No one ever left the Family except to marry, and how could she leave the father of her child? Even as Francesca pondered these questions, she knew that she would have to take the potion soon. With every moment she could feel the life rising up in her. She knew this child was hers!

But how could she trust her lover? Everyone knew he had many children and had never married any of these women. Why would he marry her? He had never even said that he loved her. NEVER! But Francesca had never said that she loved him. Maybe she didn't. Maybe she loved "loving" him, but she didn't love him. How could she wake up every morning to a man she didn't love? But then who was she fooling? She would not find him in her bed, but rather, in everyone else's bed. Right where he had always been!

Now he was telling her of a job he had across the valley, one in which he would receive much gold for gentling many horses. He would return and give her the most beautiful wedding the camp had ever known. What was happening? This was like a bad dream. There was no solution. Francesca could not have the child, and yet, she could not deny it life. She could not marry him, and she could not stay single. She couldn't even run away. She had no skills. Even if she did, who would hire a pregnant woman? Why had she not thought this out? Why had he not told her? He was experienced, and she was just a child.

In acting like a woman, she had proven herself to be a child. She had not thought or planned. She had gone after what she wanted without any thought of the consequences. Francesca needed to get away to think. At last, a little too late, she wanted to think.

He ran back to the camp now to share his "joy" with the family and probably to bed another woman. He would lose interest in her quickly now. He had owned her. He had left his seed that claimed her as his and made her dependent on him.

Dependent, like her mother was on her father. Pregnant, like her mother was until she grew too old. And Francesca had watched her mother grow old very young. When that happened, her father had searched the camp and the countryside for younger, more beautiful women to prove to himself that he was still young, even though his wife had grown old. Then he would come back and punish her for not being like those other women. He would shame and embarrass her and force himself on her. If he were drunk, which was often, he would beat her as well.

Francesca knew that her moans of joy would quickly turn to moans of pain if she were the wife instead of a lover. No—Francesca would not be a gypsy wife. Now was her only chance. If she didn't leave now, she would be forever trapped. With this thought, she began to run. She didn't look where she was running and she didn't care. She only had to run away--away from him, from her father, from the Family, and from herself. But alas, as hard as she ran, she could not leave herself behind. And, she could not run away from the fact that she was pregnant!

For days Francesca wandered through the woods. Her life as a gypsy had trained her to live off the land. Because it was spring, she found edible roots, fruit, and occasionally trapped a rodent or caught a fish. She stole bedding from a clothesline, cooking utensils from a porch and told fortunes for flour, sugar and salt. Occasionally, she slept in barns. She was surprised at how well she did for herself. However, soon she would not be able to cover her "condition" with a shawl, and the weather would turn against her. Spring would turn to summer, summer would turn to fall, and then fall to winter. She had ended her life before it had begun. The very first decision she had made on her own had nearly destroyed her.

Francesca was surprised that the Family had not found her. Perhaps, they had not looked. No one there really loved her. She was only the product of another dutiful mating her mother had performed to avoid a beating. She was only another mouth to feed, and, at best, another hand to do the work. Everyone was probably glad she had left, one less husband to find and one less woman to worry about.

Before Francesca knew it, autumn had come. As the days grew cooler, her stomach grew larger. It was more and more difficult to find food, and the farmers were too busy preparing for winter to care about her fortune telling. She found herself cleaning, milking and harvesting in order to get bread. The work was hard and backbreaking, but at least she could get some food and sometimes sleep in a barn.

But why had he not found her? Her "lover" had probably kept on running into the next county after he had told her he would love her forever. He had probably had many lovers since that evening she had left and put many other women into the same position she was in. He told her that he would love her till she was fat and old and would give her twelve children, but he couldn't even look for her when she was a few miles away, alone and with child. What was she thinking? What would be the benefit in him finding her? Now that she had run away, he would be doubly cruel. No, she was better off without him, without anyone, except the child.

She had grown very used to her son. Yes, the baby was male. Francesca had met him many times in her dream state. Her son was doing remarkably well considering the poor nutrition that she gave him, but he was determined to have life. He spoke to her in her dreams and told her that he, too, did not wish to have a gypsy's life. He had bigger plans and promised her that something would happen to save them. But, time was running out. The nights grew colder and the food more difficult to obtain. Soon the farmers would be closed up for the winter. Everyone would be snug in their safe homes with fires lit and the doors locked. There would be no work and no extra food for her. She would be completely alone. No one would take her in, as she was now obviously pregnant.

It was time. Her son had offered hope, but she could not find it. Francesca could either die slowly and painfully, or she could die quickly by her own hand. At least then, it would be over. She did not regret the loss of her life; it had been of little value and of less happiness. As for the child, she was deeply saddened she could not offer him life. She felt sure he was a powerful soul. Given a good start, he would have accomplished much, but she couldn't give him that start. She could not even carry him to full term because she would die before he could be born. Why make them both suffer?

Francesca wandered around aimlessly looking for a way to end her life. A high cliff? But the land was flat. A fast river? But she was an excellent swimmer. Poison? But she did not want to die slowly or hurt the child. A weapon? She did not possess one. Perhaps she could get caught stealing? But she did not know what they would do. They might not kill her, or worse, they might kill her very slowly. No, it must be by her own hand. It was the only way to make sure death would come quickly. She was saddened, however, to deprive the child of his life. He deserved a chance, even though she had lost hers. What to do, what to do?

Francesca walked without direction for several days. She had lost all bearing of time and space, ate little and slept less. Soon the child would die, and then the decision would be made. At last she found a deep lake. It would be difficult to drown herself because she was a good swimmer and her instincts would work against her. Perhaps she could swim and swim until she became too tired to continue, or until she was too cold to remain conscious. The water had always been her friend. It would be a good way to die. She had always listened to the water. It had shown her its face and had shown her the truth-- the truth of her small meager life. A life wasted in a few months of passion.

Francesca had hoped her life could have some freedom. She had watched the other women in the gypsy camp and seen her life spread out before her. She knew she would have until her first child was born to be free, and then she would be a virtual slave. But she never knew she would feel this way about the baby. This baby was different. He was special.

Sometimes two insignificant people can create something significant. But what was she thinking? She must end this now before there was any more suffering. As she stepped into the water, she heard a voice and the racing of horses' hoofs. Before she knew what was happening, powerful arms reached out, carried her struggling form to the shore, and gently sat her down on a fallen log.

"What do you think you are doing?" he said, as he wrapped his cloak about her. "The water is icy and you are obviously with child."

"Yes," she said. His pulling her from the water released her pent up emotions and now she was sobbing. "I am with child, but without husband, home or family. I have survived the spring, summer and fall, but I will not survive the first snow and the baby will not be here 'til winter."

He pulled his cloak around her so sweetly that she looked up from her tears and looked him in the face. His hair was pale as wheat, and his eyes as blue as the morning sky. His eyes were not young, but they were very kind. The lines in the corners of his eyes showed years of laughter and the wrinkles in his face showed exposure to the sun. As she looked closer, she now saw sprinkles of gray hidden among the yellow hair. But his "feel" was young and gentle and he looked at her as if he cared. No, no man would be concerned about her. No man would save her or even care about her. As these thoughts were going through her head she heard him say,

"How could you end your life?"

"It is not difficult to end my life, for I am worth nothing. My son, however, is very special. I have met him in my dreams, and he wants to live. He can be an important man someday and he wants a chance to fulfill his destiny. But what do I have to give him? I am a gypsy--alone with nothing and no one. I cannot offer him the life that he tells me he can have. I think that from where he lives now, he has forgotten the harshness of life on Earth. I will soon join him, and then I will have to make amends to him for not allowing him his chance."

The man crossed his arms over his chest and held his jaw in his hand. His eyes stared off into nothingness, and Francesca could almost hear him thinking. His face looked like he was trying to make an important decision. Perhaps he was the one to save them she pondered. No--what was she thinking? There was no saving her, and the sooner she accepted that, the sooner she could carry out what must be done.

"I can help you," he said in a voice so sweet and gentle that she could hardly hear it. "I am also alone, though I do have a home and a family. I have been gone for several years. I am a merchant, and I travel to trade with other lands. My life has been busy and exciting. I never married, as I was seldom home. Even though I have bedded many women, none have claimed me as a father. I fear that, in all my success, I have failed in the most basic of a man's duties. I am old now, and this is my last long trip. I also believe that your son is special and I know that you were courageous to leave the only protection that you knew. I have heard the stories, and I know that the life of a gypsy wife is unfair. I would offer you a much better life. No one would know the child is not mine, and I am too powerful in my community for anyone to shame you for being a gypsy."

What was he saying? Was he offering to care for her or to marry her? No, that was not possible.

"Will you marry me?"

Francesca snapped her face towards him and looked him straight in the eyes.

"What did you say?"

"I asked you to be my wife. I only ask that if you decide to leave me, which you may do as I am growing older and could almost be your father, promise me you will leave your, no--OUR, son with me."

She felt in her heart the wisdom and kindness of this man and knew she could trust him. The curse of always "feeling" the truth had never failed her. Francesca had always known when people had lied to her, and when the truth was spoken to her, which was seldom, she recognized it.

The child was right; someone had saved them. She kissed her rescuer gently on the lips and softly replied, "I will never leave you!"

It had been ten years. Francesca had created a life for herself. Even though her husband was as busy at home as he had been on the road, he was always soft and gentle with her. He was a constant companion for the child. He gave him everything and spoiled him horribly, but he was a good father. He disciplined him, when needed, in a gentle and firm way she had never known existed when she was in the gypsy camp. He was more the child's father than if he had planted the seed in her.

It took her years to settle into her new life. Although her husband loved the boy much more than her, he was always kind and bedded her with a surprising passion for a man of his age. He had told her that he could not father a child, and he had been right. Giving birth to her son had been difficult for her, so everyone assumed that she was the reason there were no more children. She gladly carried the blame. He had saved her and her son and had offered them a beautiful life, so it was the least she could do. She had taken his name, his home and his God.

This new life was sweet, comfortable, and secure, but it was very limiting and very lonely. Francesca spoke to her husband only about matters of the house or the raising of the child. The child was cared for by servants and educated by tutors, who left her little responsibility for him. In fact, she hardly knew him. He seemed like someone she could never have given birth to. He was calm in emotion like his "father", did everything to please him, and greeted his mother with a proper hug and a kiss.

Francesca had almost died when she gave birth and was ill for a very long time. Therefore, her mother-in-law took over most of the nurturing of the infant. She had insisted that it was not proper or "civilized" for Francesca to nurse her own child, and she had been too ill to insist. She had accomplished what she had intended. She had saved the child! But she had no value once the child was born. She had used almost all her life force to keep the child alive while she was pregnant, and without the baby inside of her, Francesca saw no reason to carry on her meager life. However, the man stayed by her side day after day. Whenever she was conscious for even a brief moment, she would see the man's loving face feeding her broth, propping up her pillow, or just holding her hand. Maybe it was the look of deep concern on the man's face, or maybe it was the feeling of love that emanated from his heart, that called her back to life.

The physicians did not know why Francesca had lived, just like they did not know why she had been so sick. But she knew! She was sick because she had no reason to live, and she got well because the man had given her a reason. But by the time she was well enough to care for the child at all, it had been almost a year. The man's mother had become the child's mother, and the man had become the child's father. And, as soon as the boy could talk, her husband had become the primary parent. Her husband had always been kind to her, but Francesca assumed he was grateful to her for his son and that she was almost dispensable. How quickly she forgot the look of deep love and concern on his face when she was sick. Or perhaps, she had just imagined it in the hallucinations of her fever.

Francesca had been married five years when her husband's mother, the matriarch of the house, died. Then Francesca became the mistress of the house. Her husband's mother had been stern and suspicious of her, but lavished the child with all the love she would not give to his mother. Perhaps her husband's mother had suspected the truth, but she didn't seem to care. There was a son in the house, and the family name would be carried on. Her other children had died at an early age, or were killed in war before they could take a wife. This baby was the last hope for the continuation of the family name. The matriarch was grateful for the baby and had asked no questions, except with her eyes!

In spite of all that seemed wonderful, a discontent began to grow within Francesca. Her life was comfortable, her son was healthy and intelligent, and her husband was attentive. However, everything and everyone was somehow a little distant from her, or perhaps she was distant from them. It was as if that early experience in the gypsy camp, and her wandering pregnancy, had created a wound within that would not go away and continued to create restlessness in her. She did not understand this. Perhaps it was her gypsy blood or her early years of moving around that made it difficult for her to stay in one place. Perhaps it was because she was so different from everyone around her. Her husband was correct. The community had respected him so much that they dared not question his choice in taking a wife. Besides, she had always been reputable and carried her new family name with honor. Francesca went to mass every day and stayed close to her house and family. She was the hostess for their many traveling guests and ruled their large home with an efficiency that she did not know was in her.

But where had her youth gone? Had she had but one short spring of excitement and the rest of her life was to be filled with discipline and responsibility? All of her gypsy instincts and skills had to be hidden, for they were considered heresy in the eyes of the church and the good people of the community. She could not go out in nature alone, or anywhere, as it was unseemly for a lady, even the matriarch of a fine house, to go about the world without a chaperone.

Since Francesca had taken on the duties of the house after the death of the matriarch, her relationship with her husband had grown into almost a business agreement. Although their lovemaking was occasionally passionate, and always kind, she felt little warmth. In fact, there was no warmth or excitement from anyone. She was an island. And the island was getting old.

The restlessness grew. Francesca found herself sneaking out into the surrounding woods and running barefoot through the trees. This act was very dangerous, as a woman of her station would never leave the house without a chaperone or without being properly attired. People would talk and her behavior could cause embarrassment to her husband. But danger brought in that element of excitement which she had so missed in the last decade. And the warmth she never found in people was re-discovered in nature. Her instincts began to return and her dream life became very vivid. Her dreams warned her that a great challenge would come to her. A challenge which could change her life—or ruin it. The danger was very clear, and she loved it. She loved the fear, because at last, she felt alive. All the comfort and sweetness of the past decade had almost suffocated her. It was so foreign, and besides, she didn't believe that she deserved it.

Francesca had done something very stupid and had been rewarded. The only thing that eased her guilt was the boy. She could hardly call him her son now. He was such a special person and her husband was so obviously happy with him. But she didn't fit. In order to appear that she belonged there and to give her son a chance to become the man she knew he could be, Francesca had to hide her true self and act as if she were someone else. But she did not know that someone else, and her true self was dying. She could feel her vitality leaving her as it did when she had been so ill.

The only thing that saved her and replenished her was her walks in the woods. More and more, she took these walks; and, several times, she even went naked. She knew that she had to stop this. The church was the center of their community, and she knew that they had accepted her because she had become a member and had gone to mass everyday. But if they found her walking in the woods with no clothing, they would consider her a witch and burn her at the stake, and her husband and son would be greatly shamed. How could she take such a risk? How could she cause such danger to the only two people in her life that had ever loved her? Yes, they loved her, but it was in a formal and gentle way that she was not comfortable with. She knew they loved her and even respected her, but the truth was, she did not respect herself!

Respect was something that she really didn't deserve. She almost became angry with them for being so foolish as to respect her. What had she done to gain it? Yes, she had "played the game". Francesca had stayed faithful to them and acted the necessary roles that their world demanded. But she missed her world. How long could she act? Her dreams warned her that the danger was drawing closer and she felt an increasing restlessness and excitement.

Then one day it happened. It was early in the morning and Francesca was returning from her obligatory morning mass, dressed in the appropriate black. Morning mass had become representative of the part of her inner battle that embodied home and family. She had spoken to the Priest about her inner discontentment, without telling him the reasons why. He had been kind and understanding and told her that she must pray. So she had tried to pray. She had prayed to Mary and she had prayed to St. John. She had even tried to pray to the tortured statue of Jesus hanging mournfully on the cross. Francesca received nothing. She could understand their sacrifices, but she could feel no joy in their presence. She only felt suffering from them. This did not help her restlessness, and in fact, created even more.

This morning, she prayed with special fervor because she felt her challenge was near. Strangely enough, she had found some comfort in mass that day. She could almost feel what her challenge was, but was afraid to know. As she was walking up the stairs to her door, a tall man also dressed in black walked swiftly towards her and said,

"Francesca?"

At first she thought he was a merchant friend of her husband's and wondered why he had addressed her in such a personal manner. Then she saw his face. It was he--her gypsy lover. She felt completely overwhelmed by an array of conflicting and intense emotions. An alternate reality stood before her. What if she had not run away? Or, what if he had found her? What if she had aborted the child or even, she cringed to think of it, she had actually taken her life? As these thoughts flooded her mind and fought with the many conflicting emotions, yet another reality seemed to enter her mind. The world around her seemed to stop. The gypsy man stood still with her name still upon his lips. The bustling town was completely still and as quiet as death. Perhaps she had died. Perhaps the shock was too much for her and it was her heart that had stopped rather than the world around her. Deep inside of her the memory of a distant place gradually dawned. She could feel an intense struggle as some part of her fought to be alive, to be heard.

* * *

Inside the dome, Shature struggled to awaken herself from the illusions of her Earth reality. The young, innocent maiden's desperate search for love had trapped Shature in earthly emotion. She fought to remember how to call her Guide, and to regain her objectivity and detachment.

"Please," she called from deep inside her torment, "help me!"

Slowly the chair lowered, and she gradually began to "see" her Venusian life. She felt the presence of her Guide. He lovingly held her hand and wiped away the tears that Shature now felt upon her face. Yes, the pull from the physical was strong.

"And so were the emotions of that life." replied her Guide, who was responding to her thoughts.

"Oh, dear Guide, how can I return to the third dimension again? I am not ready. I cannot even 'view' this life without getting lost."

"Dear Shature, what was it about that life that so trapped you?"

"I don't know," Shature mused as she gradually recovered some degree of detachment. "Francesca was so young and innocent, and all she wanted was to be loved. But she felt abandoned. Abandoned by her parents, by her gypsy lover, by the man who married her, and even by her son. She felt so alone and, in order to survive, Francesca had to sacrifice who she truly was."

"But didn't Francesca run away?" questioned the guide.

"Yes, she did. She had to. She knew that no one cared for her. She ran away so that she would not have to face the disappointment that she knew would follow if she stayed."

"How did she know that she would be disappointed?" asked the Guide.

"I don't know," cried Shature as anger rose up in her. "I guess she ran away because she was afraid."

"Afraid of what?"

"Yes, yes, I see where you are going," Shature said angrily. "She was so afraid of being abandoned by her lover and her family that she left them first."

"So, she was afraid of abandonment, then she was afraid to trust her lover, and then she became angry," continued the Guide.

"And then she became someone she was not because she was afraid that she could never be loved for who she was. Why, this is the pattern that was started on Atlantis! Oh, dear Guide, will I ever heal that initial pain? Will it follow me into every incarnation?"

"Ancient pain that was created on the third dimension is best healed while in that dimension. This will be your challenge when you return to Earth. Pain and sorrow are part of the illusion of separation. The limitation stems from your first experience of separation from the Oneness and your resulting feelings of abandonment. These patterns of behavior are played out again and again until the Soul is healed. As you offer guidance and unconditional love to the third dimensional selves that you are viewing, you are assisting them in changing their lives. Then, when you take embodiment again, your 'past lives' will not hold so much pain, your emotional body will be clearer, and it will be easier for you to hold more light, recognize and accept your Divine Complement, and fulfill your Soul's purpose."

"But why is there the illusion of separation on the third dimension? Why can't we remember who we are when we have a physical form?"

"My one, you ask a very difficult question and one that is best answered by you. And in each life the answer may be different. However, I can tell you that the illusion of separation is what allows the incarnate persona to experience the most individuation from the higher worlds of the Oneness."

"But why would we want to be individuated from the One? No! Allow me to answer that question."

Shature took a moment to go deep inside herself. She closed her eyes to shut out her exterior world and took slow, deep breaths while she concentrated her attention on her third eye. Just as she could guide her lower dimensional realities, she could be guided by the realities that were higher than her own. A golden star appeared in her inner vision and a feeling of euphoria entered her being. In a moment of no time, she knew the answer.

"We are like the seeds of a flower that fall from the safety of Home onto the earth so that we can learn to be flowers ourselves."

"Yes, and the time-space continuum of the third dimension allows the 'flower' to learn the effect of its thoughts, emotions, and actions. Action and reaction are very slow in the third dimension so that it is easier to learn. Here, in the fifth dimension, the results of one's thoughts and emotions are instant," added the Guide.

"Since we are living in Oneness here, every thought and feeling can be felt by all. We would never have a harmful thought or action against another because there is no separation between us. Anything we do to another, we also do to ourselves," Shature concluded.

"Do you see, Shature? You are enjoying being independent. You want to find your own answers inside of yourself. You have gained that trait by your incarnations on the third dimension.

"But, you must return to Francesca now. Do not abandon her. She is on the verge of hearing you, and she has a major decision to make. Her greatest fear has been that she shall forever lose herself to a world that she doesn't understand and cannot embrace. However, how can she leave her son and the man who has saved her life?"

"Yes, I understand. I think that I can help her now."

Shature lay back in her chair and signaled for it to be raised again into the dome. As she entered it, she saw Francesca frozen in time before her with a look of confusion on her face.

Shature instantly took pity upon her and merged with that life, this time careful to maintain her objectivity. Shature sent her fifth dimensional love into Francesca's heart and her higher vibrational thoughts of comfort and assurance into Francesca's mind.

"It is I, Francesca, a higher component of yourself," Shature said telepathically as she stood before her, a wispy form of light.

Francesca crossed herself and reached for her rosary.

"Be not afraid. I know that those rituals have brought you comfort in the long and lonely time since you have given up the beliefs of your youth. Think of me as an Angel if you must. It matters not how you call me. It is only important that you listen."

Francesca appeared calmer, and she replaced her rosary in her small bag. She had heard Shature's words and was realizing how much of herself she had lost. Shature could read Francesca's memories of her youthful communion with nature and the Spirit world. With those memories came a great sadness.

"My youth is gone forever," spoke Francesca. "I am a matron now, alone and lonely. This gypsy man is my last chance to revive the portion of myself that I murdered that day by the lake."

"Oh, Francesca, you are wrong," assured Shature. "You shall be young again and again. The life that you are now living is only one of thousands of lives you will live to allow you to grow into a full awareness of your Self. Now your only concern is that you make this decision from love!"

"From love of whom and of what?" asked Francesca. "Do I love my husband and my son, do I love this man before me, or do I love myself?"

Shature could feel the confusion in Francesca's mind as she replied. "Love is contagious. If you can love even one of those people, then eventually you will grow to love them all."

"But I am afraid that I will make the wrong decision and spend the rest of my life paying for it."

Francesca was starting to cry.

"Allow love to ease your fear. Any decision made in love is better than any decision made in fear. Feel the love that I have for you and the love that others have for you as well."

"But no one else loves me," cried Francesca.

"Are you sure of that, Francesca? Are you sure?" Shature said as she faded from Francesca's vision.

*   *   *

The world around Francesca slowly returned. Into her awareness came the noise of the busy town, the wooden rail, which she grasped tightly in her hand, the cool breeze and the sound of her name from a familiar, but different, voice. Francesca's encounter with her higher self quickly left her consciousness. But the feeling of love remained. Love for her son, love for her husband and even love for her gypsy lover. But most surprising of all -- she felt love for her self.

"What are you doing here?" Francesca heard herself say in a calm and caring voice.

With a silent and controlled passion, his eyes reached out to her and he replied,

"I have looked for you for many years. And then, last week, while camping in the woods nearby, I saw you walking, alone and barefoot. At first I didn't recognize you. You carried yourself with such an air of confidence and dignity, and you were dressed like a fine lady of wealth and name. I probably wouldn't have even looked twice had you not been without a chaperone and without shoes. I was so enchanted by the paradox of a fine lady walking in the woods alone, like a gypsy, that I followed you. It wasn't until you sneaked into your house like a servant that I got a good look at your face and recognized that it was you, my Francesca. At first I thought you worked in that house, but the way you carried yourself and dressed was not the way of a mere servant. Now I have discovered that you are the mistress of this fine house."

Francesca was shocked and pleased by his words. She had never seen herself in those terms. In all these years, she thought she had been acting; but if she was, how could she have fooled even him? He had known her intimately as a passionate and frightened young girl. She was so surprised by her reaction that she could barely speak. When she did speak, she was even more surprised by what she said.

"Yes, I have made a life here and a happy one at that. I have more than I knew existed and I am loved and cared for deeply."

Was she lying to impress him, or was she telling a truth she could never accept before?

"We can't talk here," she continued, "it is indiscreet. Please come inside. I will greet you as I would one of my husband's merchant friends. You, too, are dressed and behave in a manner quite different than I remember."

He smiled and nodded his head in response to her compliment and followed her inside. Once in the door, she beckoned the servants to provide him with food and drink in the main parlor. She excused herself to go upstairs to change clothes and to collect herself. What a fool she was to let him in, but she couldn't send him away. This was the challenge she had been awaiting and she must face it head on. Her husband was in the next town for a week, and it was not uncommon for her to greet his associates in his absence. This was another point of strength that she had not noticed about herself until now.

When she returned to the parlor, she poured herself a cup of tea from the serving that the servants had placed before her guest. She had collected herself and calmly sat across from him.

"Can we talk?" he said.

"Softly," she replied.

"When I first realized who you were, I wanted to take you with me. I had suffered guilt upon leaving you, which greatly surprised me. I had left many women, and many had borne my children. Although I escaped you, I could not release you from my mind. Your touch and "feel" haunted me. Your soft laugh and quick humor was a memory I couldn't escape, and you had listened to me in a way that no other woman had, or for that matter, has to this day. I looked everywhere I expected you to be, but you were nowhere. At last, after many years, I came to believe you were dead."

"I almost was," she replied, "but I was rescued by a man with a kindness and understanding that I had never known existed."

At this point, a young lad of about ten years rushed into the room to hug and kiss his mother. Maybe for the first time, Francesca realized how proud she was of her son. He was more affectionate than she had remembered, too. He communicated with her in a loving and intimate manner that she had never before recognized. Why did her life seem so beautiful today when just yesterday uncertainty and discontentment tore at her? From the corner of her eye, she saw the gypsy carefully eyeing the boy. She could tell that he knew it was his son. However, she would deny it to her death. The boy had lived with and loved her husband for so many years that he had even grown to look like him. In his love for her husband, the boy had adopted many of his postures and mannerisms and even seemed to have his temperament. No, this was a secret she would guard with her life. She had done one thing correct in her life. She had married her husband to provide her boy with this life, and she would never risk having anything harm them.

In an instant, she recognized her challenge. She could be wild and free, and almost young, traveling as a gypsy. She could even have other children if she wished. But she knew she never would!

"This is a merchant friend of your father's," she said to the boy. "I'm sorry, sir, but I have quite forgotten your name. This is my son and the heir of this household," she exclaimed proudly.

The gypsy understood everything that sentence meant. He introduced himself to the boy, and they made small talk while she sat back and realized the importance of this day. She would tell her husband, of course, when he returned home. Her ex-lover stood and said that he was sorry to have missed his friend, but he must be on his way. Perhaps he could drop by the next time he was in the area? The boy said his good-byes and ran to his room while Francesca slowly walked her guest to the door. She gave him her hand, which he kissed. Before he left, he looked longingly into her eyes, then suddenly turned and was gone. She knew she would never see him again.

The next morning she awoke a different person. The restlessness and dissatisfaction were gone. Although the woods still beckoned her, she now would take a chaperone, perhaps her son, and she would wear shoes. The town seemed friendlier, the church less threatening, and she missed her husband. How could such a small occurrence create so many changes in her? How could one small decision change her entire attitude on life? She took her final walk alone in the woods, with shoes on, to think this over.

Perhaps it was because someone from her past, the main someone, had seen her as such a different person. She had always thought she was acting, but even he was convinced. Maybe, when she thought she was acting like the lady, inside she was really acting like the gypsy. Maybe a change had taken place in her that she could not understand until someone who had known her very long ago had seen it.

But why was the dissatisfaction gone? Her life now was exactly as it was before yesterday, except for one major difference. The decision she had once made out of desperation, she had made again out of love. Yes, that was it! Since she made this decision out of love for others, she could begin to love herself. And, as she made it out of respect for others, she could respect herself.

Francesca felt a wave of love wash through her total self. For a brief moment she thought that she saw someone watching her. Yes, just behind that tree. No, it had just been her imagination, but the feeling was familiar. It was a feeling of love coming from herself to her self. This love expanded and embraced her son and her husband. She could feel now how much they actually loved her, and, yes, how much she loved them.

Francesca realized that she couldn't wait for her husband to come home so that she could say to him again, this time out of love and respect,

"I will never leave you!"

* * *

Shature was crying again as the chair lowered, but this time her tears where not of pain, but of joy.

"I remember now how wonderful human love was--and how difficult. Maybe it was the extremes of emotion that made love in the third dimension so enticing."

"It is true," agreed Shature's Guide, "that the third dimension is very alluring. However, it is difficult to maintain the same objectivity of opposites there that you have from this dimension. You have seen how easily your emotions can trap you in a situation and cause you to forget your greater self."

"And I have also seen how the fear of something actually creates it. The truth was that no one abandoned Francesca, even her gypsy lover. But, she—I—was so afraid that I would be abandoned, I couldn't trust that those around me actually loved me. I was afraid to love and afraid to trust that others loved me."

"But when you sent your fifth dimensional, unconditional love, to Francesca and she was able to accept it, her healing began. From feeling the love from you, her own Higher Self, Francesca could also begin to love herself and acknowledge the love of those around her. In that one moment, her whole experience of life changed. What could have been another great disappointment and challenge became a moment of awareness--awareness of her Higher Self and a better future. Then she could acknowledge her own accomplishments and raise her self-esteem.

"When her self esteem was raised," continued Shature, "Francesca could release her fears of abandonment, trust that her husband and son loved her, and return that love to them. Unconditional love received from a higher portion of her self allowed her to break the pattern of abandonment, mistrust, and anger."

"But, who was Lamire? I had thought that he was the gypsy, but Francesca chose her husband so I guess he was Lamire," pondered Shature.

"Oh no, Shature, your Divine Complement was the gypsy."

"Do you mean that Lamire was there, right in the eyes of my beloved gypsy?"

"Yes, Shature, but you could not believe that you were worthy of such a great love. You could not believe that you were more important than the other women he had been with."

"Therefore," continued Shature, "I ran away from what I truly, deeply wanted because I could not recognize it. What I really wanted, more than a conquest, a sexual experience, or my freedom, was LOVE. I even tried to run away from the consequences of my actions by ending my life, but my unborn child would not let me die. This child of our love, Lamire's and mine, had to live. I chose my husband because I chose my son. He was a good man, and I could not hurt my son by leaving him. I had to finally take full responsibility for my actions so that I could learn to love myself. Then, someday, I could love myself enough to recognize Lamire and allow myself his love."

CHAPTER THREE

COURAGE

"In the next reality you will view, you are again a woman. This time you are born in a time when the whole world is locked in a battle for survival. Love and hate intermingle, as hate makes the bonds of love stronger. It may be extremely difficult for you to maintain your objectivity as you view this reality. Do you think that you are ready, or would you prefer to take a rest?"

Shature thought for a long moment before she answered.

"I appreciate your warning, but I want to continue. I think that I am beginning to understand how I can observe and merge with my third dimensional realities without becoming trapped in their illusions. I wish to try again. However, is there a way in which I can call for your assistance without leaving the dome if I feel that I am losing my fifth dimensional awareness?"

"Most assuredly, just call upon the Violet Fire. The Violet Fire is the signature frequency of this temple and is of a vibration that will restore your fifth dimensional awareness and perspective. It will also help your third dimensional self release the illusion that is causing discomfort, and allow him or her to feel your presence."

"Then I am ready," said Shature confidently. She calmed herself and lay back in her chair as it rose into the dome. She was determined to keep her fifth dimensional perspective no matter how strong the pull from Earth.

* * *

Poland, circa 1940

It was raining and cold. The weather was threatening to make her late for her appearance, and the damn Nazis were everywhere, checking papers, checking IDs. Why were they checking her? Illiana was the one who had always lived here. They were the visitors, or rather, the invaders.

Illiana must not miss this performance. It was very important. Her dance troupe was going to make a statement. It seemed like too many others were placidly accepting the invasion of Poland and carrying on with their lives as if it didn't matter. Some people seemed glad.

"Now something can be done about this awful economy," they said, as if the Germans cared about Poland's economy. Poland was a part of the Germans' economy. They were the first bite of the German pie. The Nazis had come to eat them up, take all they could and leave the crumbs for the citizens who had spent generations here. Her family had been in Poland longer than anyone could count. And for several generations, they had been in show business. One of her first childhood memories was of the Stage Master lighting the stage footlights. She would sit in her playpen, stage left, and watch him prepare the stage for the evening performance. She had learned young that if she were very quiet, she could sit in this place all evening instead of being whisked off to a dressing room. Her parents had learned, very early, that if they let her stay there, she would be quiet all evening and gradually fall asleep by herself. Her goal was to see the stage master put the footlights out, but she seldom achieved this until she was much older and out of the playpen.

The rain was making the traffic so difficult that she was tempted to get out and walk, but she was worried she would be "detained" by one of the soldiers. Many of her friends had been detained. Some returned, but many did not. None of her Jewish friends returned. And she had many. Her heart ached for them. No one knew where they were taken or why. Her friends were performers like herself. They harmed no one and, in fact, they helped ease the fear and sorrow of the time.

Tonight, her dance troupe would give a special performance in honor of their missing friends. They had a mime planned at the end of the third dance which asked some important questions. They knew it was dangerous to do this, but wasn't it more dangerous to do nothing? Besides, they could all be "detained" for doing nothing. So if they were to be taken off to who knows where or what, at least they would have the dignity of knowing why.

At last, she was at the theater. She quickly paid the cabby, grabbed her bag and ran to the rear stage door. She reached the dressing room just in time, but found only half of her friends there.

"Where is everyone?" she asked.

"Some are too afraid to do tonight's performance, and some are just missing. We don't know who is what. We only know that this is it and we must go on stage soon."

They all talked about their fears, and all but two decided to go on anyway. The two decided to leave because they had children to consider. The seven who were left were single, and no one else would suffer from their actions—they hoped.

The performance went well, but the consequences were greater than any of them could imagine. Before they knew it, without questions, trial, or a moment to tell anyone, they found themselves stuffed into the boxcar of a train and taken to a distant and dismal location. What they saw there was too awful to describe.

Before she could understand what was happening, Illiana found herself in surgery, awake and very aware, as some form of experiment was being performed. She didn't know which was worse—the pain of being in surgery without anesthetic, or the humiliation of having a circle of men watching while others took out her feminine organs. With so much blood, one would think that she would pass out or not notice the others watching, but this was not so. She was in combat with these evil men. She would not cry and she would not pass out. At every available opportunity, she looked them in the eyes, and she ranted and raged at their stupidity until, at last, they gave her ether to shut her up. She got her full power that day. Perhaps that is why she did not die.

After her operation/torture in which she saw them take her womanhood, she bled and bled. The Nazi "doctors" tried experimental means in which to stop the bleeding, but nothing worked.

She was glad. There was no reason to live. Why should she try to recover? However, the bleeding did eventually stop, and she did not die.

Later, when she was well enough, she was transferred to the soldiers' entertainment area. However, the entertainment she was forced to offer was NOT dancing. She did dance, but she was then taken "upstairs" by whoever chose her. Night after night, her body lay passive while her mind created a cave that they could not enter. Her secret was that even though they could do what they wanted to her body, they could not touch her mind. This is what kept her sane -- and ANGRY. When she was recovering from their "experiment" she had tried to die, but she could not because her anger kept her alive. She was too angry to let them destroy her, too angry to let them win. When she was a child, her parents had often reprimanded her for her temper and competitiveness. Now it kept her alive, and in Hell. She knew then that she would have to plot her escape in earnest. She would have to find an ally.

"I won't die, so I have to get smart and make one of these jerks MY captive," she chanted over and over.

Women had been captivating men for centuries. However, as long as she was an ugly lump of passive flesh, she could not captivate anyone. The thought of enjoying being with these excuses for men was abhorrent, but she was an actor. She would act—something else women had been doing for centuries. First, however, she would have to bait her trap. She rummaged around among the clothes of the people who had recently been killed, the best of which had been sent to the soldiers' canteen, and found some appropriate clothing. With alterations here and there, she made herself some costumes. There was lots of make up, also stolen she was sure. She did her hair and made up her face. However, she was far too thin. The Germans liked their women filled out, and she had to please the audience. She would have to start eating.

On her debut night, she was dressed to kill -- literally. She came into the canteen, appropriately late, and walked over to the piano. She gave some tunes and her key to the piano player and began her act. Somewhere in that "audience" was her prisoner. She scanned her quarry. She needed someone who was able to leave the camp regularly, perhaps, someone who went to France. She had heard that they had an active underground there. Yes, she would need an officer or a pilot. Since she was not Jewish, they had put her in the officer's canteen. What did it matter? She would never bear them a little German bastard. Therefore, the pickings were good because the room was filled with the men in power—until she pulled them, or rather him, into her web. She would have to find someone who wasn't too repulsive. She wasn't *that* good an actor!

And then one night Illiana spotted him, or did he spot her? Actually she felt him before she saw him. His gaze was so intent on her. She had been on her "campaign" for several months by then. She had gained weight, her color was back, and her hair had regained its luster. Anger was a good medicine for her! As she finished her song, she looked into his eyes. Something caught in her throat as they made their connection, but she refused to view him as a human. He was an animal, like all the other Nazis. He was a means to an end, nothing more. She would use him as the Nazis had used her. Having fully convinced herself of this fact, she turned her head and bowed to the crowd. As several men came towards her, she turned her back and busied herself at the piano. She put out her feelers to sense if he was moving towards her, but she felt nothing. Oh well, she thought, this is only the first night. But as she turned to leave, she bumped right into a giant. Her head was far below his shoulders, and as she looked up, she saw that it was he. She couldn't help but see the medals that he wore. He was an officer and a pilot. Perfect! But what wasn't perfect was the feeling that she had when he stood so close to her.

"Good," she thought, "I won't have to act so much."

He didn't say a word. He didn't have to-- she was a whore! He silently led her upstairs. He allowed her to take the lead as they reached the walkway of the mezzanine, so that she could guide him to her room. As she entered the room, she lit the candles before she shut the door. She had sneaked around for months to find things to turn her cell into a room. She refused to think about what she had to do to get someone to bring her candles. She had also gotten some paint from another "friend" and had painted murals on the walls. Over the bed was a tree. In fact, it was a tree from her childhood. She would stare at it when she began to lose control of her "act", and it grounded her. As a child of the theater, she knew well how to set a stage. She had hung beautiful fabric, which had once been a dress, over her excuse for a window. She had even found a rug for the floor. The trap was set! She would make him fall in love with her, or at least in love with what she did for him.

He began to undress her without saying a word. This was definitely the silent type. Even though she was short and small, he would have been huge next to any woman. She wondered if he would be too big for her, but then, one size doesn't necessarily match another. She would definitely find out soon enough. The chemistry between them frightened her, but she knew that it was the best bait of all. These kinds of sensations were not unilateral, especially when she hated him as he probably hated her. Good! Hate is extreme anger, and anger was her friend. She allowed him to take the lead, and at the same time, she remained aloof and almost condescending. She could tell that this attitude excited him. He was a pilot, a thrill seeker. She would have to make sex as dangerous as flying a plane in combat. Luckily, she had been thinking about this a lot and had many plans. When she was down to her bra and panties only, two important parts of her costume that she had to give another girl a black eye in order to get, she pulled away. She saw the look of shock and excitement on his face as she did so.

"Are you this big all over?"

She managed to give the impression of looking down at him at the same time as she had to bend her neck to look into his eyes.

He smiled, still no words.

Illiana went to a box, which she had carefully covered with material, in which she hid her props. From it she pulled out two crystal glasses and a bottle of cognac.

"From a friend," she said, aloofly.

She also grabbed a silk scarf which she draped over her shoulders. The colors of it highlighted her dark brown hair and green eyes.

"Also from a friend?"

His first words.

She ignored his question.

"Would you like a drink first?"

He nodded and sat down on the bed. She came very close to him as she filled his glass. Now his head was below hers. She liked that. She filled her glass, allowing her silk scarf to touch him as she did so. She had sprayed it with perfume that she had stolen, another prop. She carelessly allowed a bit of the precious liquor to drip. She slowly and deliberately licked the neck of the bottle.

"This is very special. I save it for special times. It would be a shame to waste a drop, don't you agree?" she said in her best German.

She had learned many languages as an actress, and it had been a great advantage to her to know what the soldiers were saying. She would use this advantage to the maximum. She put the bottle on the floor and then put the lid on her prop box, pulling it over to the bed. She set the bottle and the glass on top of it.

"I can dance very well," she said aloofly. "I will take the rest of my clothes off by myself."

She would ask nothing of him.

"Drink," she directed.

As she hummed a tune, she took down her hair and fluffed it with her fingers. She laid the hair clip on the box beside her glass. She picked up the glass and took a long slow drink, peering over the rim of it straight into his eyes.

It was working. He was staring, his breath short and erratic.

"Aren't you warm? Let me remove your jacket and boots."

She slowly undid each button on his jacket and lingered long in unbuckling the belt on his coat. She pushed the shoulders back from his chest as she allowed her breast to come very close to his mouth. She pulled off his jacket and carefully hung it on a hanger attached to a hook on the wall by the door. She knew how much the Nazis treasured their uniforms. She straddled his leg, carefully allowing him a view her behind and pulled off his boot. She had had much practice with this maneuver. Before her "campaign", she would allow them to take her with their boots on. This was rape. If she had to be a whore, she would be one that they had to respect. She knew how to do that, because German or not, they were all men!

With the second boot off and placed carefully in the corner beside his jacket, she began her dance. She used the scarf in many unusual and erotic ways as she slowly and carefully removed her prized undergarments. She sang softly the entire time.

When all was removed, save the scarf, she walked over to him. She leaned over and kissed his neck as she began unbuttoning his shirt. Her mouth followed the trail down his chest as she opened his shirt all the way down to his belt. She undid the buckle and stood back. On cue, he stood up and removed the rest of his clothes. He tossed them on the floor. A good sign. She was more important than his uniform, at least for now. He picked her up like a doll and she wrapped her legs around him. She could feel him against her. It was as big as the rest of him. He put her back up against the wall and put himself inside of her.

"I am bigger than you may think," she whispered in his ear, and he was gentler than she could have thought.

She would have to be careful not to enjoy it too much. She had to stay in control and remember that she was a prisoner, and he was her jailer. As the evening continued she would forget that fact for the passion between them wiped all thoughts from both of their minds. When at last they fell asleep, intertwined upon her small bed, it was dawn. Yes, she would have to be careful.

After about an hour, he arose from the bed, kissed her lightly on the forehead, and dressed himself. As he opened the door he caught her eyes and said,

"I will see you again!"

"How do you fit yourself into that small cockpit?"

"Just like I fit into you," he whispered, as he bit at her breast, "I adapt."

Their lovemaking had indeed been as dangerous as flying a plane. They had made "love" everywhere, in the hangar, on the roof, under the piano and in the fields nearby. She had even slipped into his barracks, with his help, of course. Since she was with him, she could go many places that she would never have been allowed to go otherwise. And she was WITH him!

When he found out that another man had forced himself on her while he was on a mission, he beat the man within an inch of his life. After that, everyone else left her alone. She sang and entertained while he was gone and entertained him while he was there. The situation was almost bearable. Being with him was not bad, and sometimes, even though she could not admit it, it was actually very good. She had to be careful not to become caught in her own trap. She was a prisoner. If he died, which he very easily could, she would be exactly where she was before she had met him. In fact, it would probably be worse. She had made many enemies by his favoritism. She would have to plot a way to leave soon.

"You know," she cooed. "The only place we haven't done it is in the air."

"I think the distraction would be dangerous to our health," he laughed.

"I don't mean when you are on a mission. I mean when you're on a trip to a meeting or something, perhaps on your way to Paris. I could do anything that the French whores do, even better. I'm all yours, and when I moan, I mean it!" she lied.

"I don't think they would be too happy about my taking a prisoner out of the camp."

"But, I would be your prisoner," she said as she began to seduce him. "How do you think this would feel at 15,000 feet?"

She showed him how it felt on the ground. She didn't push the issue, she just dropped the idea now and again when he was most likely to listen to her. She stepped up the lovemaking even more. She made him feel like the most wonderful and important person in the world when she was with him. Anything he wanted she would give him. Luckily, she was a good actress and luckily, he was gone on a regular basis because her body was damaged from her surgery.

The constant submissive attitudes mixed with role-playing kept her from falling in love with him, and sometimes even from liking him. She was a non-person. She was his fantasy, a reflection of his desires. Illiana had become a Nazi's dream!

At last the day came. He was going to Paris for 48 hours. She would also have to entertain his C.O. and wondered who he was, but she hid her feelings and showed him her excitement and gratitude. Luckily, she had been saving pills. She would have to take some before the flight to numb herself.

The plane flight had been horrible. Thank heavens for the pills. He had locked her in the room while he was at his meeting; not that she had the energy to go anywhere. She had to rest and save her energy for the evening. She had a plan. He was taking her on the town that night; she would prove to him that he could trust her. And then, late that night, before his return flight, she would drug him and sneak out into the street.

It had worked! He was asleep and drugged in the room and she was actually leaving the hotel. She had crept down the back stairs and left by a fire escape into the alley. She had no idea where she was, she just began running down the alley away from the hotel. She didn't know where she was going, but she kept her eyes open and her instincts tuned. It had started to drizzle and small puddles were forming in the holes of the cobblestone street. The buildings were wet and gray and rose high above the narrow streets. The sky was thick with fog and visibility was poor. She rounded each corner very carefully, searching for German soldiers. And then in the distance, coming towards her, were two forms. In the fog, she couldn't tell if they were Germans, but their heavy foot falls and military walk told her that she was in trouble. Just to her right was a small all night restaurant. She walked into it quickly, hoping they had not seen her.

Her terror must have shown on her face because as soon as she entered the door, a small man grabbed her by the arm and said, "Come with me." He called in French to his helper, who ran to the door and began mopping the floor where she had entered, to cover the puddles that came from her shoes and clothes. He then put up the chairs and made a display of cleaning the restaurant. The other man took her through the kitchen, into the pantry, and through a secret door at the back of the pantry.

"Go down the stairs and be very quiet. I will come down when it is safe."

Luckily, she spoke enough French to understand him. As she went down the stairs and around the corner, she saw a small light, a short table, a small wooden cot and a tall pile of blankets. She took off her wet coat and shoes and hung her coat on a peg. She kept her shoes close by in case she had to run and wrapped herself in several blankets. Maybe she should prepare herself to run, but somehow she believed that this was the safest place.

One of her few friends in the camp had lived in France before she had been taken prisoner and had told her about the French underground. Hopefully, that was where she was. She had grabbed a large bottle of pills before she left, and if she were captured, then she would take them. Even with these few moments of freedom, she knew that she would never allow herself to be captured again.

She froze as she heard German voices and heavy footsteps above her. But she also recognized the small Frenchman's voice laughing and conjoining them in broken German.

"You are late tonight." he said. "We thought you would not be here and were cleaning up. Come, sit."

Illiana heard him yell at his helper in French to put down the chairs and get their food. No wonder he had spirited her away so fast. The two Germans she had seen were regular customers at this restaurant. Had they been there at their regular time she might have bumped right into them. She surmised by their casual talk that they had not seen her. She had been slinking along the walls of the buildings, careful not to make any noise with her footsteps. Even though she felt relatively safe, she quietly put her shoes back on. She dared not walk to her coat for fear she would make a noise. There was no window or other visible escape from this room, so she held the bottle of pills in her hand with the lid off. She heard the door open and someone coming down the stairs. Just about to empty the contents the contents of the bottle into her mouth, she saw that the Frenchman was alone. He rushed to her with reassuring words and took the pills from her.

"No, no, you are safe. This is the underground."

These were the last words she heard before she fainted.

For three weeks, Illiana was barely conscious. Her fever was so high that she hallucinated, and she came to the edge of death more than once. It was as if the truth of which she had become in order to survive and escape was so awful that she would almost rather die than face it. This time, there was no anger to rescue her. She was safe and in the care of warm, loving people. She couldn't face life again and she couldn't die, so she lingered. She lingered in the area of her consciousness where she wasn't dead-- and therefore did not have to face her maker--and also wasn't alive—and therefore did not have to face herself. Previously, she had survived because of anger; this time she survived because of love. Not her own love, but the impersonal love of the Frenchman and his wonderful family. She had become their "niece" who had traveled from the south to be with them, and the cold, rainy weather of Paris had made her ill.

Finally, one day, after drinking a bowl of warm broth carefully spooned into her mouth, her eyes fixed upon the holder of the spoon. She was a short round woman with gray hair and warm brown eyes. When "Mama", as everyone called her, realized that her patient was finally awake and aware, she put down the soup, almost spilling it in her excitement, and threw her arms around her ward as if she were her long lost daughter. Yes, she would live now! She would leave her horror behind and face a brand new life. There was love and caring. There was, after all, a reason to live.

As soon as she was physically able, Illiana became involved in the workings of the underground. The neighbors and the Germans had accepted her as a family member and she was free to move throughout the neighborhood. The underground had created papers for her while she was sick, and her French improved rapidly as she spoke only that language. Apparently her pilot had been too embarrassed or worried about his own name to mention her disappearance. At camp, she would be reported as escaped or dead. However, she would have to be very careful not to run into the pilot or his C.O.

For that reason, she stayed inside as much as possible and disguised her appearance with a shawl, glasses and country clothes when she went out.

Perhaps her pilot was dead. Was she happy or sad about that? She didn't know and decided not to think about it. That was another life, one that had been burned out of her in the weeks of fever. Her health was still delicate and she often had pain where her female parts were supposed to be. She wondered if that were psychological. She didn't care. She knew that she wouldn't live much longer and knew it. It would be nice if she could experience love at least one time before she died. Real love, not enslaved love like with the pilot, or impersonal love like with Mama, but true man-woman romantic love. She was selfish to want so much. She should be grateful that she was alive and free!

And then, one day it happened. She was bringing food to one of the underground hiding rooms when she met another pilot, but this time he was British. His name was Lieutenant Stephan Ferguson and he was from Cornwall. The second she saw him, her heart skipped. He didn't notice her though because he was barely conscious. A farmer had found him half dead in a field in the countryside. His plane had been hit over Germany, and he was trying to limp his way back home, but the plane couldn't make it. He thought he might have passed out from his injury because all he could remember was suddenly finding himself off course and plummeting towards the ground. He barely had time to parachute out before his wounded craft crashed. He was able to bury his chute and limp some distance away from the crash before he found some cover in a small cave and passed out.

A farmer found him while searching for firewood and had notified the underground. After days of traveling and hiding, he had finally found his way here. He, like Illiana, had recognized the true severity of his injury when he finally felt safe. He was fighting a bad infection in his leg where he had been hit. Luckily, the bullet had gone clean through, but the bone had been broken and the lack of adequate care during his flight to safety had made the injury life threatening.

So now it was her turn to be the nurse. She cared for Stephan day and night. She helped hold him while they set his leg and she constantly cleansed his wound and changed his bandages. From his fevered ravings, Illiana learned that he had been shot down before. He didn't know where he was and didn't recognize her from one day to the next. Her heart went out again to the

Frenchman and his family when she realized the amount of dedication that it took to care for a critically ill person. She was grateful that she had a chance to pay back their kindness to someone else.

She knew that it was ridiculous to fall in love with someone who didn't even know that she was there. For all she knew, he had a wife and family. But her life since the Nazis had invaded Poland had not seemed real. It was like a Greek tragedy with one awful event following the next. Any moment that she could steal a feeling of happiness, even if it was an illusion, was a moment worth risking death. She would also willingly die for the man she had come to love. If she could surrender her worthless life so that he could live and work toward the end of this horror, she would do so without blinking an eye.

But she didn't have to die. He was getting better. His fever finally broke and his wound stopped oozing pus. They had threatened to cut off his leg in order to save his life, but she, as a dancer, had fought them.

"There are things worse than death. This is a pilot and a young virile man," she cried. "Perhaps he would rather die as a hero than live as a cripple."

She found out later that she had been correct. He thanked her profusely when he found out that she had not let them amputate his leg, and that it was only her constant vigil that had finally won out over the infection. Maybe it was also her love. If hate can kill, then why can't love heal?

Illiana had never had much of a relationship with God. In fact, she had been furious with Him since she had been captured. She had been raised as an agnostic, but suddenly developed a belief in God when she had needed someone else to hate. For this wounded man, however, she had prayed even though she had never even prayed for herself. She had offered her life in exchange for his, more times than she could remember. And now he was better. He would live, and he would keep his leg. Was it God who had saved his life, was it her love, or was it his will? She would never know, but she thanked God anyway, as He was the only one she could thank.

During his long convalescence, she came to him several times a day to care for him, read to him, and bring him food. She would drop her shabby disguise before she went into his underground room, brush her hair and put on whatever makeup she could find. Her cover was that she delivered bread, what there was of it.

This activity gave her a reason to go to different homes. After she left him, she would wipe the make up off her face, pull her hair into a bun, and put on her shabby coat, glasses and shawl. Transformed back into her mousy, shy cover, she continued on her delivery route.

Illiana didn't want to admit it, but she actually felt happy. She was, unfortunately, also afraid-- afraid that she would get caught and afraid that she would die. Yes, for the first time in years, she was afraid of death instead of wishing for it. She had a reason for her fear. She realized that her body had felt this way since the surgery, but it was worse now. It was as if, when she allowed her to feel happiness and relief, she also felt pain and foreboding. Maybe this was because she was no longer numb. When she was in the camp, she didn't allow herself to register any sensations outside of those that may lead to her escape. Now that she had escaped, all these hidden feelings rushed to her consciousness at once. Unfortunately, part of her did not return from her last brush with death. A part of her had died after her first near-death experience, and there was not enough of her left to survive another journey into the land of the beyond.

Perhaps, that was why she had been thinking about God. She started this relationship to save the Englishman, but now she was continuing it to save herself. Not to save herself from death, for she knew that was inevitable and imminent. No, she continued and expanded her relationship with God because, if there were one, she would meet Him soon. Maybe He did accept her bargain of her life for the Englishman's, though He was kind enough to let her live a little while before she had to pay up. No, that was superstition. She was thinking like a gypsy. Lives were not to be bargained for like a bushel of wheat. She was just frightened, especially frightened to believe that she may actually be happy.

Each day Stephan got better, and each day she fell deeper in love. She kept her shameful past a secret. She told him only that she had been in a camp and couldn't talk about it, and he respected her wishes. They didn't talk about the war or what had happened to them in it. Instead, they created a fantasy where it didn't exist. They talked about their childhood, their interests, art, philosophy, and eventually, they talked about love. They didn't carry their love into the future, nor did they discuss any loves they had had in the past. They kept true to their fantasy of now. Now, they were falling in love. Now, they were holding each other. Now they were making love.

Yes, they made love often -- sweetly, kindly and intimately. Her lovemaking with him erased all her bad memories of who she was, and what she had done in the camp. When she made love to him, they reached a spiritual union she had never thought was possible. Because of the desperation of the times, or possibly because they both knew that it couldn't last, they cherished their time together all the more. Or, maybe, they were just deeply in love. In her fantasy, it was the last reason. In her fantasy, all was well with the world. Time only existed when she was in his arms. In his arms, she forgot the past, she forgot the war, she forgot the danger, and she even forgot the pain that was increasingly growing deep inside her body. He was like a drug for her, and she was a drug for him. Not an addictive drug, but a healing one. Neither one of them were demanding or needy. They had both come so close to death that they were simply enjoying this moment of life!

Unfortunately, their love made them more daring than wise, and he did need fresh air to complete his healing. Besides, it was difficult to confine such passion and lust for life to a small, dimly lit room. They began sneaking out of the room and going out to the countryside. Their actions were dangerous to more people than themselves, but they had to take the chance. The Underground had made him papers, which he carried, but he spoke no French, and looked far too English. Illiana had two people who knew who she was and who may even be in Paris, but all went well—for a while.

They had had a beautiful day in the countryside. They had found a cave above a lovely valley with trees covering its entrance, and had enjoyed a picnic at the mouth of the cave. They made love for dessert--again and again. Before they knew it, it was almost dark and time for curfew. How were they to know that there had been a military action in the countryside nearby, and that the entire area was teaming with Nazis? Unfortunately, they were far too exposed before they realized this. They were stopped again and again. Their papers were checked and they were examined. He was "deaf" and could not hear them, or respond, and luckily, her French was much better. They made it all the way back to the city, and then he saw her. In her love and joy, she had not donned her mousy garb. She had been so terrified by all the examinations that she did not cover her head and change her hair, as she usually did. Just about the time that she thought she was safe, she heard him calling her name.

Illiana recognized his voice instantly. How could she ever forget it? She froze, not knowing what to do. Then she quickly pushed aside her lover and ran. She knew that he could not follow her, as he could still only walk very slowly and carefully using a cane. And she knew that if she ran, the Nazi would follow her. Fortunately, she had learned the small streets like the back of her hand, and even though he was faster, she knew where she was going and eventually lost him. When she was sure it was safe, she made her way back to their cellar room. Stephan was there and frantic for her safety. They held each other tightly and made love desperately. They knew that it was almost over.

Illiana also knew that her Nazi pilot would stop at nothing to find her now. She could endanger the entire Underground network if she were to selfishly hide within it. Worst of all, her lover would have to be moved to another location away from her. The Nazi had also seen him, and she knew that nothing would stop his jealous search. She was dead. She just did not know how or when.

* * *

Suddenly the entire room filled with a brilliant Violet Light. Illiana looked to Stephan to see if he saw it too, but he was fast asleep. The light became brighter and brighter until Illiana could see nothing else.

"I am dead now," she thought, "but how did I die?"

"You are not dead," replied a voice that was sweet and clear.

Illiana blinked her eyes in the hope that she could see the source of the voice, but whoever was speaking remained invisible.

"You are not dead," the voice repeated. "You are experiencing a moment in which you are free of the illusions of your reality."

"Illusions? I don't know what you are saying. There are no illusions now. They have died with my fantasy that I could have a normal life. I have harmed everyone who has cared for me because I imagined that I could find love in the midst of this hateful war. I was wrong. There is to be no love for me, only pain—more and more pain."

Illiana now lost all control and began to sob as she buried her face in the bed sheets. Then she felt something like a touch. It felt like the wings of an Angel were wrapped around her. She did not understand what was happening, but it felt good. So good, that she actually allowed herself to fall into the feel of it. She continued to cry, but now there was a source of comfort. Invisible arms were gently holding her as she leaned against an invisible shoulder. The presence was feminine, no it was masculine, no—it was both. It was a presence that was beyond human, yet seemed to understand her very human sorrow.

At last her tears were spent and she was ready to listen, and the invisible voice continued. "It is true that you will die soon, my One, but there is one more valiant deed that you must do."

"What do you mean by 'one more'? I have not been valiant. I have been terrified."

"Yes, but one can be terrified and a coward or be terrified and brave. You, my dear, have been very courageous. And there is one more courageous act that you can do to save your Stephan and your friends in the Underground."

"Oh, please, tell me what I can do. If there is any way in which I can correct my mistakes, I will."

"Dear, you have not made a mistake. You merely wished to experience love. All will be fine if you continue to make your decisions from love."

"What do you mean?"

"Love shall set you free!" said the presence as its voice faded with the Violet Light.

"Wait! Wait! I don't understand what you mean. Come back. Come back."

* * *

"What is wrong, dearest?" Stephan was awake and holding her. "You were having a bad dream. Come, lay down with me again. All will be fine."

Illiana lay down and allowed him to hold her, but she could not go back to sleep yet. She was still a little frightened and very confused. What she had just experienced was not a dream. It was real. But what decisions did she have to make and how could she make them from love? Her mind whirled with a million possibilities until, gradually, the memory of the Angel's arm and the Violet Light calmed her and she drifted into a dreamless sleep. When she awoke she knew what to do.

"It's too dangerous to travel as a couple after he has seen you and me together." Illiana told Stephan the next morning. "You must go to a new location at once, and I will follow you later," she lied to him.

It was hard convincing him, but by the next nightfall he finally gave in. He would leave with one of her friends in the Underground at dawn inside a delivery truck hidden among crates and boxes. This was their last night together, but only she knew it. They were closer than they had ever been. She held his heart within her soul. By dawn, she was ready. They made their plans of when she would meet him, and she lied convincingly. She walked him to the door and they kissed their last goodbye.

"We shall be together again. Nothing will stop us!" She said as she looked deep into his Soul.

"Nothing," he repeated. He kissed her one last time, turned and left. She closed her eyes and felt his kiss again; it would have to last her for the rest of her life.

She didn't know exactly what she planned to do, but she knew that she was a danger to everyone. She had not told the truth to Stephan, but she was confident that she had done the right thing—the loving thing. The violet being said that she would die soon, and she knew it was true. She would only be an encumbrance to him and diminish his changes of escape. As she watched the truck drive away and the sun begin to rise above the rooftops to the east, she remembered the Violet Light and the Angel's touch. She felt strong now; she knew what she had to do. She could not stay where she was and endanger the wonderful people who had saved her, and she could not subject herself to further imprisonment or torture.

Illiana would have to go away where she could die alone. Already she felt the familiar pain from her "surgery" like a hot knife in her womb. She had to clinch her teeth to stand up straight. But first, she would have to warn her friends in the Underground so that they could prepare. They had been so good to her, and her selfishness had greatly threatened them. She walked as fast as she could to the home that served as the Underground Headquarters. It seemed like a lifetime ago that she had run terrified into the restaurant on the ground floor. Somehow she disguised her pain long enough to tell the man who had once saved her life what had happened. He went to her and lovingly put his arm around her.

"You are right, you are already associated with us and the damage may already be done, but we may be able to find a safe place for you to hide."

"No," she cried. "I will not endanger you any longer."

The thought that she could cause harm to her friends coupled with the feelings of her loss of Stephan made Illiana forget the Violet Light and the Angel. She ran from the room before he could tell her of his plan. She did not know where she was going, or why. Her entire life was ending and she had also endangered the few people that she had loved. She had done the loving thing, but it was too late. She ran randomly through the small streets until the river loomed up before her. Yes, that was the answer. As she ran towards the river, she felt the warm blood dripping down her legs. Whatever was wrong with her was indeed much worse. Surely God would not see this as suicide, but only the shortening of an inevitable end. She was so consumed by her own agony that she didn't notice the dark form to her side. She was crossing to the bridge when he grabbed her.

My God it was him -- her Nazi. How had he found her? How long had he been following her? She was too spent to struggle, and when she caught her breath to talk, all she could say was,

"Please God, don't torture me. I am dying."

What she heard in return was more shocking than a bullet between the eyes.

"Torture you, how could I? I love you!"

The shock of what he said was too much for her. She collapsed into his arms.

When she awoke, she was in a small apartment, and he was caring for her. There was no strength or will left in her. She saw in the corner of the room a trash can filled with bloody towels.

"I can't stop the bleeding," he said. "And if I get you help, they will turn you over to the SS. My C.O. found out that you did not return to the camp, and he is furious. Only, I think, because he wanted more of you. I have been looking for you to warn you."

She had lost so much blood by now that she was barely conscious. She looked through a blur of consciousness and into his eyes.

"I won't come back this time. I don't have the will or the reason. I have hurt or endangered everyone I have ever loved, including you."

She was surprised by her last remark. How could she love him? He was a Nazi. He was everything she had grown to hate and fear. As she looked into his face, she recognized a tenderness in him that she had refused to see before. He leaned over and gently kissed her forehead.

"We are losing the war now. Soon France will be liberated. I, too, will soon be dead. All the high officials are gathering their money and going to South America. I have been demoted for allowing your escape, but I don't care. I can't kill anymore. I must tell you that you have loosened something in my heart that I never knew was there. When you left me, I was so surprised at my response I could not even be angry. I missed you terribly. But I could not blame you. Deep inside my heart, I was glad you escaped. I never thought the war would go this way. I loved my fatherland, but the atrocities I have seen have disillusioned me more than I can stand."

She could barely hear, or believe, the words he was saying. He was actually humble and kind. She wanted to put her arms around him and kiss him one last time, but she did not have the strength. In fact, she found she could not even talk. The room around her began to blur, and she felt a strange tugging on her body. Illiana was frightened, and at the same time, she was joyous. Suddenly, she felt a release and then she saw her body below on the bed, in a pool of blood. He was leaning over her sobbing. A Nazi fighter pilot was sobbing at her death! She felt a surge of love for him and then the room began to fade.

* * *

When the chair came to the floor of the circular room, it gradually returned to a sitting position. Shature was silent for a long moment, as was the Guide.

Finally, Shature asked, "I see what you meant about love and hate and the struggle for survival."

Shature was silent then, waiting for the memory of her earthly emotions to calm. At last, she said, "Dear Guide, even from here I am confused. Did Illiana love or hate the Nazi pilot?"

The Guide smiled and lightly touched her on the shoulder. "You did well in maintaining your connection to your fifth dimensional perspective," he said, avoiding her question. "It was indeed a difficult challenge."

Shature smiled and a short laugh escaped her, "Without the Violet Fire, it would have been impossible. It also helped Illiana as you had said. She was—I was—able to send Stephan away so that he could be safe. But was he safe? Did he escape?"

"You know the answer. It was your life."

"Yes, that is so," reflected Shature. "But why don't I know the answers now? It seems like when I am in the dome observing and assisting my other realities on a lower dimension, I am somehow in touch with an even higher portion of myself. I know that it was I who held Illiana and comforted her, but I do not have wings. However, in that moment within the Violet Light, I felt those wings about me and a consciousness within me that far exceeds the person that I know as myself now."

"It is often in assisting others that we help ourselves."

"Is that also true for you, my Guide?"

"Of course," he responded as his aura beamed and filled the entire room.

"Now Shature, there is more to this life. Return to Illiana. She has died to her physical form and is upon the fourth dimension. When you return to her, call upon that essence within yourself that is of a higher vibration. Lay back upon your chair-- Illiana awaits you. Just as I am your Guide, you are hers."

Shature obediently lay back in her chair and re-entered the dome. She had never helped one of her third dimensional selves after death before. She was curious and a bit anxious. As she entered the dome, she saw Illiana in her astral body.

* * *

As Illiana left the room, she saw above her a tunnel of light. It pulled her in and she began to whirl around as she moved forward. She heard many sounds of bells and flutes. Beyond the tunnel, she saw images of her dead parents and her many dear friends who had died or "disappeared" in the war. Was she dead also? Or was she truly alive for the first time?

As she floated past each of these people she felt more and more detached. It was as if they were from another time and place, and she had no inclination to communicate with any of them. Illiana then entered into a warm, golden glow that seemed to be emanating from above her. Gradually, she began to make out a form within the light.

"Who are you?" asked Illiana, but she did not really say the words. Instead, her thoughts floated out of her ethereal body in wispy strands of light.

"My name is Shature. I am your Guide," the figure replied.

Shature was a radiant being dressed in iridescent robes with a friendly, reassuring smile.

"I know you. You are the one with the wings who held me when I was so afraid. Where am I? Am I dead?"

"You are in a place of evaluation in-between lifetimes, where you have an opportunity to learn and grow from the life you just experienced. Follow me," continued Shature while she led Illiana into a beautiful green garden filled with lovely flowers, trees, waterfalls and streams.

Illiana followed. She did not know what else to do. She had never heard of such a concept as "in-between lives". When she was alive, for she now assumed that she must be dead, she had never studied spirituality and had begun to relate to God only at the end of her life. Even though she had thought often about her death, she had never dared to think that there might be something after it. Maybe she wasn't dead. She knew that she had been very, very ill. Perhaps she was hallucinating.

"No, Illiana, you are not hallucinating. You have indeed died to the body that you have known. However, life itself is continuous and does not die. It only alters form. The form that you now inhabit is your fourth dimensional body which is made of a higher vibration than your physical form," Shature said as she directed Illiana to sit upon a marble bench beside a stream.

Illiana looked very confused. In fact, she was so confused that she could not even ask a question.

"I am sorry," continued Shature. "I have forgotten that you have just left your third dimensional body and are still attached to that way of thinking. You are now in what your world has known as Heaven or afterlife. However, the afterlife is not just a different place. It's a different dimension. It's the fourth dimension. Upon this dimension is the record of all the thoughts and emotions that you experienced in your life as Illiana. You will soon enter a Mystery School where you can learn about that life and prepare for another one."

"What is a Mystery School?" asked Illiana.

"A Mystery School is a place in the higher dimensions where you can learn about your Soul and all the lives that it has experienced."

"Is this place a Mystery School?"

"Yes, in a way it is. Actually, it is what you might think of as a waiting area. There are certain understandings and detachments about the old life that must take place before you can actually enter the Mystery School."

"I am really dead," Illiana said almost to herself.

"I know that the end of your life was filled with fear and struggle, and you had no time to reflect. Therefore, many of the things that I say to you may be very confusing at first. Would you like to begin by asking me questions about the life you have just left?"

"Yes, I do have a question. I want to know about something that happened before I died."

"I will help you if it is permitted. Since we can read thoughts here, I can see that your question is about Stephan."

"I want to know if he escaped."

"Yes, he did."

"Please, tell me more."

"Are you sure you want to know? It might upset you."

"Tell me anyway, please."

"He did escape, or will escape, depending on your time perspective. Yes, I see I have confused you again. Time is not the same here as it is on the Earth plane. What can feel like a few moments here, can be years there, or vise-versa. That is why I may not be able to answer all of your questions. Stephan has escaped and has returned to England via a fishing boat. There is another mission on which he will be asked to go. If he takes this assignment, he probably will not return."

"Then I must tell him not to go on that mission. I must stop him. Can't I talk to him as a ghost or something?"

Shature smiled in a deep and loving way.

"That would hardly be detaching from that life, now would it?"

"But I can save him!"

"And what will you save him from? From his right to make his own decisions?"

"But he doesn't know that he will die on that mission."

"He had to face death before every mission. He has already cheated death twice."

"But this is different. This is not a gamble. This is a sure thing."

"My dear, you are not a member of that existence anymore. You cannot intercede in his decision making if you wish to continue in your growth. And, as you see for yourself, death is not a bad thing. It is merely a transition from one reality to another. He and his Soul will determine which reality he is meant to exist in at this 'time'. You are still holding on to your old physical thoughts. Perhaps there is a reason that you are not aware of why it is best for him to cross over."

"I can't understand why someone would willingly want to die," she lied.

As Shature looked at her, Illiana immediately felt embarrassed for her untruth. And, more importantly, she understood how she and her Soul had decided it was best for her to cross over at that "time". She had survived a very difficult experience, escaped it, and had helped others to escape as well. She had even had a wonderful love affair. But then a picture crossed her mind.

One that she did not understand. She saw herself in a room, tied to a chair, and Nazis were beating her and putting out cigarettes on her body. With fear and confusion she looked to her Guide.

"That was an alternate reality," Shature said, answering Illiana's unspoken question. "Whenever one is at a crossroads in his or her life, an alternate reality is created for the path that the person did not take. However, these crossroads are only from choices that one can conceive of. For example, Stephan, your lover, is about to be at such a crossroads himself. He will have an opportunity to make this important flight which can help in determining the course of the war. He knows that it will be very dangerous. If he accepts the mission, he will probably die. If he does not, then he will return to his home and an unhappy marriage. His wife has been sleeping with a neighbor, thinking that Stephen is dead. But, in fact, the relationship with the neighbor started shortly after Stephan left for the war. Whichever choice he makes, there will be an alternate reality in which he can live out his other choice."

"When you chose to run away from Stephan on the night that you were discovered coming from the countryside, you made an unselfish decision which set into motion the reality which you just experienced. In an alternate reality, you stayed with Stephan and you both were captured and interrogated. That is the vision that you saw."

"And," Illiana interrupted, "there is a reality in which I did not send Stephan away without me and warn my friends in the Underground, and they were captured as well."

"I can see that you are beginning to understand. In the reality in which you just left, your friends in the Underground are all safe."

"Thanks to your kind intervention," added Illiana. "I am glad that I made my decision from love and that no one was killed or injured because of me. In the other realities, am I dead or am I alive?"

"Dear, you are never dead. However, in some of your alternate realities you have died and in some of them you are still alive."

"I can see that I will have much to learn in the Mystery School."

"Yes," Shature spoke as she pointed to two angelic beings who had just appeared. "I believe that you will soon be ready."

Illiana rose, as did Shature. They embraced each other and Illiana turned to leave, but before she did she turned again to Shature.

"Will I ever see Stephan again?"

"Yes, you will, in some reality.

* * *

"I had forgotten about alternate realities until I began to instruct Illiana," spoke Shature as her chair came to a stop on the floor of the circular room.

"Yes, alternate realities spin out from your third dimensional life during a time when there is more than one choice as to how to proceed," instructed the Guide. "Each conceivable choice can become an alternate reality. However, if one cannot conceive of, or imagine, a certain choice or action, then it will not become an alternative reality. In other words, if you cannot imagine that your life can be filled with love, then that reality will not be created. That is one of the ways in which you are assisting your third dimensional selves. Your intervention allows them to conceive of a reality filled with love rather than fear. If they can believe that love is possible, then they can create a reality filled with that love."

"So when I reminded Francesca and Illiana that they could have love in their lives, they were then able to create that reality."

"Yes, that is true," smiled the Guide. "Souls tend to respond in the same pattern over and over until they are able to connect with their Higher Guidance and remember that love has the ultimate healing power. If they can feel the love within and around them then they may not fall victim to old patterns. These old patterns of behavior were created as a mechanism to cope with fear.

"Your coping-mechanism to deal with the fear of abandonment, Shature, has been to withhold trust and to then be angry that you could not trust others. This pattern was created because it protected you from trusting someone who might abuse that trust and hurt you. However, your lack of trust also disallowed the possibility of someone being trustworthy.

"Do you see the pattern of abandonment, fear of trusting, and anger in your life as Illiana?" asked the Guide.

"Well," Shature thought for a moment, "Illiana was not abandoned by a person, but she was abandoned by her world. She had a happy life as a dancer and actress until, suddenly, and seemingly beyond her control, everything that was dear to her was taken away. She was, of course, afraid to trust, as there were many enemies. Her coping-mechanism was to mask her fear with anger, and it was that anger that kept her alive. Then love healed her anger and finally brought her happiness.

"It was Illiana's fear of how she might harm her loved ones that called me to her aid. Because she could hear my words and chose love over fear, she created a reality where she died peacefully by the side of one who had loved her. Interestingly, the one who loved her was the same man whom she had once hated. In addition to the Violet Fire, I think that it was Illiana's force of love that saved me from becoming trapped in her emotions."

"It was also the force of her love that allowed Illiana to raise her consciousness enough to perceive your presence. Because she could feel love, even though she was also feeling fear and remorse, she was able to gain assistance from you, a higher portion of herself.

"Do you think," the Guide continued, "that Stephan might have felt abandoned by Illiana. After all, he never learned that she had died."

"Oh no, I had not thought of that. But wasn't it a good and loving thing to send him away?"

The Guide merely smiled in response.

"Stephan was Lamire, wasn't he? I have just viewed two lives in which I chose to leave my Complement."

"That is correct. But when you ran away from the gypsy, it was from fear and unworthiness; and when you sent Stephan away, it was with love and unselfishness."

"When I was in the dome, I could not tell if Stephan or the Nazi pilot were Lamire. I felt an instant recognition for both of them. I would think it would be easier to recognize my Divine Complement."

"On the contrary, the emotions of the third dimension often make it very difficult to even recognize your Self and impossible to recognize your Complement. Also, when you were in the dome, you had to remain focused on Illiana, as well as stay grounded in the consciousness of Shature."

"But I did have a certain feeling with Stephan-- a feeling that made me want to give anything, even my life, so that he could live. But I made a vow that I would see him again and he agreed."

"Maybe he also recognized you. You see Shature; you are preparing to enter into a very important third dimensional reality. In that reality, you will be a woman in the United States of America at the close of the twentieth century. From our position in the no time of the fifth dimension, this life, like all the other lives you have observed, is in process. In that particular life, the Grand Cycle, that you volunteered to remain on Earth for when you left Venus, is ending. The planet is preparing for a shift in vibration into the fourth and fifth dimensions, and many of the Venusians who answered the call to assist Atlantis will incarnate again to assist in raising the collective awareness and consciousness of Earth."

"How will that experience be different from what I have been doing in the dome?"

"You will actually enter that physical body, like you did on Atlantis, and assist that portion of yourself to consciously remember her Divine Complement and her higher dimensional aspects."

"Will I enter that body at birth?" asked Shature.

"I am not sure. You will enter the body when it is able to hold your advanced vibration. I don't know when that will be as your earth self is creating it day-by-day. But remember, there are many parallel realities that you can access from this dimension. The Oness will instruct you as to the perfect time for your entrance into the physical body."

Shature gave a weary nod. She was having a difficult time shaking off the pain and heartache of Illiana's life. How could she actually enter third dimensional Earth again and not become lost in fear and confusion?

"I can see that there is much for you to digest. You have learned a lot. Would you like to complete this lesson?" comforted the Guide.

"Oh no, I am anxious to learn more. But you are right. I think I could use a rest."

"Then, please, go outside the Temple and wander through your beloved gardens. Allow what you have learned to integrate into your consciousness and return to me when you are ready."

"Yes, I think I will. Being in the lovely nature of Venus calms me. I will return shortly," said Shature as she stepped down from her chair and walked towards the door. Almost as an afterthought, she turned toward her Guide.

"Thank you," said Shature as she reached out to take the Guide's hand. Their eyes met. His gaze calmed her more than words as she felt a surge of his unconditional love. In response, she telepathically called on Lamire to meet her in the garden.

"You see," said her all knowing Guide. "Love is contagious."

Shature smiled and went out to meet Lamire.

GUILT

She crept from the bed that
she had allowed to become a prison.
Not a prison of love or of duty,
but rather, a prison of
GUILT.

Guilt of deeds from a time
that could no longer be recalled.

But still, the scars remained
creating an itch that
could not be scratched,
a small, subtle pain that
could not be located nor released.

How that pain had influenced her life.
How she had maligned herself,
and how she had denied herself
LOVE!

And why?
Because she remembered
the feeling of guilt.

What she had done to deserve such guilt

she did not—could not—know
for, if she knew,
surely she would be
LOST.

And so, the snake remained
beneath the rock,
where it could not be seen,
where it would not be heard.

If she crept too close,
she might remember.
And, in the remembering, would come
FEAR.

Fear of Love.
Fear of Hate.
Fear of Death.

Because once in death,
the memory would become the
TRUTH.

Could she face it?
Could she face the truth
of what she had done?
No -- Never

she must never see this truth.

Surely, if she did,
she would become insane

…or perhaps,
she may be
FREE!

CHAPTER FOUR

UNWORTHINESS

"I was wondering," spoke Shature when she returned from her walk in the Temple gardens refreshed and ready to learn more. "What happens when one chooses the path of fear and darkness rather than the path of love and truth?"

"Well, if you are ready for more, I can best answer your question while you observe from your chair. Remember Shature, once you are able to assist your third dimensional selves in resolving those polarities in their hearts and minds, they will be able to raise their consciousness into the Oness where all polarities are recognized as the edges of one perception. Therefore, do not judge your self for making the choice to experience darkness, for it is an opportunity to experience the greatest separation. It is also how your "selves" learn the consequences of selfish and fearful behavior."

Shature lay down in her chair once more and made a mental note to keep her Guide's words in mind, so that she did not judge that portion of herself who had chosen to experience fear and darkness. As her chair lifted into the dome, she heard her Guide saying,

"Listen to my voice while you view these next lives and remember the use of the Violet Fire."

As Shature entered the dome, she saw herself as a man who was riding a horse that was rapidly galloping across the moor.

* * *

19TH century England

The wind was blowing harshly and the rain pelted his face, yet he rode at a gallop. It was dangerous, as there were many places where the horse could trip and break a leg. However, the man and horse had been through here many times and they knew the path well. He knew that it was dangerous to run his horse in these conditions, but he was late. He had promised his wife that he would not be late this time. But his game of cards had kept him. When the lad had come to tell him that she had gone into labor, he had been winning. It would have been stupid and expensive to leave then, and the others would have been angry. Yes, that was it, he couldn't let down his "friends", but he could let down his wife. It was just another child. They already had five.

Why did she need him to be there at the birth? He would only be shoved off to the kitchen to drink and wait. The midwife would never let him in. That was the reason why he had been late the last three times. He only got underfoot and added to the general commotion. You see, he was a considerate person. His wife was always telling him that he was a loafer and a gambler. She nagged that he was selfish and unreliable. Well, he did the best he could. He certainly gave her a house full of children. She said she wanted that, didn't she?

Unfortunately, the rain became a deluge and he had to slow his pace to a trot. He would probably be there after the child was born -- again. But that was best, actually. Finally, as he saw the light of the house in the distance. The rain let up and he was able to make a gallant run into the front yard. He yelled for the handyman to take his horse, but he was not around.

"No good, lazy....", he muttered under his breath.

It was so hard to find good help. Well, he couldn't leave his horse sweaty and cold. He had to care for it first. It was twenty more minutes before he entered the house.

When he came in through the kitchen door, he saw no one and heard nothing. Now, finally, he was worried. He ran up the stairs to find only his wife, in bed and asleep. Or at least she looked asleep. But when he walked to her side, he found she was stone cold and her face was ashen gray. She was not asleep. She was dead! Before he could grasp the full force of this realization, he heard the voice of the neighbor woman saying,

"Where were you? She called and called for you. She began to bleed and the midwife could not stop it. Before the stable boy could return with the doctor, she had bled to death."

"Where are the children?" he asked in a stupor.

The neighbor replied, "My husband has taken them home with him. He said I should wait here for you because he would probably shoot you dead if he were to see you. The stable boy rode into town to tell her parents. I think it's wise that you leave before her father finds out. Her father never liked you, and I'm sure he will blame you for her death."

As usual he thought only of himself. He ran from the room, supposedly in grief, but, in reality, in fear. He went back to the stable, saddled his horse again and disappeared. Some say he went to London. Others say he went to America, and still others say they heard a disgruntled loser, who had accused him of cheating in cards had stabbed him in an alley behind a bar. He had done more and more of that after his wife's death. He had cheated her, cheated his children and cheated himself -- to death!

* * *

"Shature!"

The Guide's voice penetrated Shature's mind as the chair was lowering to the floor.

"I cringe at my ability to be so insensitive and selfish," Shature said, forgetting her vow not to judge herself.

"When do you think that you could have interceded in order to assist him?" asked the Guide, ignoring Shature's self-judgment.

"I don't know. I was trying and trying, but he never once raised his mind above his own selfish concerns. He could not become vulnerable enough to accept help or to ask for it."

"Are you sure?" questioned the Guide. "Observe the life again. Look for a point when he appears to imagine that there could be another way to think or behave."

***

Shature entered the dome and observed the gambler's story two more times, but it wasn't until the third time through that she saw it-- right at the end of the story, when the neighbor asked him where he had been. Was that a moment of remorse or guilt? Yes, and then he uncharacteristically asked about the children. Perhaps Shature could get his attention then. She used the Violet Fire to fill the room. The gambler did not see it, but he did seem to see her out of the corner of his eye. Shature moved into his field of vision. If she could get him to notice her, to believe in something more important than himself, perhaps he could hear her.

Shature tried repeatedly to capture the gambler's attention, but it was no use. He could not believe, even for a moment, that he had something better in himself, or that he could communicate with someone who could care enough to help him. The moment was gone and Shature could not get it back. Shature knew that the fear of the gambler's father-in-law arriving and punishing him, the way his father had punished him again and again in the cruelest fashion, replaced all his remorse. Fear filled him and all he could imagine was punishment and death.

Therefore, the only choices he could make were from fear. Defeated, Shature lowered her chair to talk again to her Guide.

* * *

"I could not help him."

"Yes, one can only choose love if they can imagine the possibility of it. If they cannot conceive of their own worthiness, you cannot help them."

"Furthermore," Shature continued sadly, "I have a feeling that my wife in that life was Lamire, my Complement. I was too absorbed in my own pain and unworthiness to accept her love. Even after the death of my wife, my Complement, all I could think of was that I would be punished. Lamire, in the form of my wife tried to save me with his love, but I could not accept it."

"Nor could you accept the help of your higher self," added the Guide.

CHAPTER FIVE

Abandonment

"I was unsuccessful in helping the gambler. Can I try again?"

"Yes. View now another similar life. Again, watch the entire story and then look back at the moment of vulnerability in which your third dimensional self is open and could possibly accept you assistance. Remember to maintain your fifth dimensional perspective which is beyond all judgment."

As Shature entered the dome, she saw that again she was a man. In this life, he was in the United States Cavalry, but his uniform was torn and dirty.

* * *

USA post Civil War

The night was very dark because there was no moon. He wandered along the rim of the desert, knowing that eventually he would have to cross it. He had avoided it as long as he could. Since he had left his regiment he had been alone, but at least he was still alive. However, if he didn't cross the desert, they would find him and shoot him as a deserter. They would never understand that he had a good reason for leaving the battle. His unit had been unprepared for the attack and before they knew it, they were surrounded. Most of his regiment had died in the battle, and he would have died too. Before he ran off, he thought he had heard his brother calling him, but he couldn't get to him to save him. What would be the point of them both dying or of him being captured? He had heard what the Indians did to their prisoners.

He still did not know how he and his horse had made it past the Indian. All he remembered was that he rode without looking back until his horse could go no farther. Then he traveled on foot for several days until he came to the edge of the huge desert.

So now he was safe. Or at least out of immediate danger. But he had other dangers. If he didn't enter the desert, he would be caught and executed. However, if he crossed the desert, he would assuredly die on the journey. Therefore, he had escaped a quick, brave death for a slow, cowardly one. With that thought, he realized what a poor decision he had made. And worst of all, he had left his brother, which meant that he could never go home. Now he had no one, he was in the middle of nowhere, and he felt like he deserved nothing -- especially life.

So why couldn't he just surrender? Why couldn't he go back, tell his Captain he got disoriented in battle, and take his punishment? Why? Because he was a coward! He had labeled himself for the rest of his life, no matter how short that may be. Well, he couldn't sit there and quiver-- he had to enter the desert NOW.

He knew that what he saw was just the edge of it and that the farther into the desert he got, the worse it would become. He had only the water in his waist canteen and he had NO food. He knew he was going to his death, and he knew he would die alone. No one else would see his shame.

He was surprised that he had survived for three days, but now the well-rationed water was gone. He had traveled only at night and slept under any protection he could find in the day. Now, he was beginning to hallucinate. For the last day or so, he kept seeing his brother and his brother was angry.

"How could you have left me?" cried the vision of his brother.

His face was sorrowful, and his wounds were perpetually bleeding. He figured that this vision was his punishment. He deserved it. So he just listened and watched. He didn't try to defend himself because there was no defense. He figured either he was hallucinating and would soon die, or his brother was a ghost and was haunting him.

By the end of the fourth day, the visions became so bad that now he couldn't sleep in the day because he would have terrible dreams. The very battle he had run from was replayed over and over again. He thought he had escaped, but there was no escape. He was beginning to look forward to his death. Perhaps then he would have some peace.

Finally, on the fifth day, death was his best friend. The wounds he suffered in the desert were worse than any battle wounds. His brother cried at him incessantly, and he relived the battle over and over in his mind. He was so afraid he would die in battle that he ran away to his death.

* * *

Shature reviewed the deserter's dilemma several times before she finally decided she needed her Guide's assistance.

"Do you need my help?" His voice was instantly in her mind.

"At least he is remorseful, unlike the other man," she responded.

"The other man? Shature, these men are you. I can see that you wish to disown them, but they are a portion of your total Self."

Her Guide was right. She was trying to disown these portions of herself. Shature realized then that she had been judging the deserter just as she had judged the gambler. She had forgotten that all of life is an experience. Shature took a long moment to think. How could she relate to these men, these portions of her Self? They were cowardly and insensitive. They cared only for themselves and they had abandoned their loved ones. She heard a warm chuckle from her Guide. Yes, that was it. The old scar of abandonment had reared itself again and confined her to a sense of anger and separation—this time from her own masculine component.

Shature summoned Lamire into her mind and heart. Instantly, she felt his reply. He was her completion, as she was his. She was as much masculine as he was feminine, and he had felt as abandoned by her as she had by him. She had not been able to find a way to help the deserter because she had been judging him.

Shature filled the dome with the Violet Fire and looked again at that life. She knew then, with great sadness, that Lamire had been the brother that had been left in the heat of battle. How could she forgive herself for such a deed? How could she have been so blind as to not recognize him? Now she was judging herself. She must forgive herself, and the mistakes she made while in physical form. The fear of Earth was great. Often poor decisions were made when fear clouded the memory of love.

She looked again at the deserter's life. There were many moments where the deserter was vulnerable enough to hear her call, but he was the most receptive when he imagined his dead brother before him. Shature decided to project herself into the deserter's hallucination of his brother. Perhaps she could convince the deserter, this portion of herself, to take responsibility for his actions.

* * *

"Do you wish that both of us died in vain?" Shature spoke through the form of the brother's ghost in the deserter's hallucination. The deserter was nearly dead and ready to accept responsibility for his actions. Heat, exposure, and his own impending death made him vulnerable enough to listen.

"Who do you suppose will take care of our Mother? She awaits our return."

"But, brother, I have abandoned you. How can I return to our mother and tell her that?"

"Do you think that one cowardly act will heal another?"

"But I cannot return. I am almost as dead as you."

"Are you sure? You have been so engrossed in your suffering that you have not noticed the nearby mountains."

"But what will I do if I get there?"

There was no response. The vision was gone. His brother had been right. He could not make up for his grave mistake by surrendering to his fear and remorse. The mountains were still far away, but they offered him the hope of a new life and a new opportunity to correct his past mistakes. Somehow he would make a life for himself and send for his mother. She shouldn't lose both her sons.

Maybe there was a reason why he ran. He would think about that as he walked to the mountains. But he wouldn't excuse himself. He would tell his mother the truth. He had become frightened in battle and left his brother behind. At least, he hoped he would have the courage to do so!

CHAPTER SIX

RELEASING THE VICTIM

"Very good," smiled the Guide as Shature lowered her chair. "But don't get too comfortable. I wouldn't want you to believe that only your masculine sides can act from their fear. However, before you re-enter the dome, I wish to remind you that the physical plane is like a schoolroom where life mirrors to you all that you seek to understand. You take on a dense physical form to experiment at being a creator. In the third dimension, cause and effect are slowed down. In this way, it is easier for you to observe and learn how you have created you life experiences by the thoughts and feelings that you have chosen to allow into your consciousness.

"These choices, or decisions, are the 'causes' of the 'effects' that appear in your life. For example, the deserter chose to leave the battlefield because he had allowed his fear to overwhelm him and because he thought that he could not save his brother. The effect of those choices was his guilt. In the case of the gambler, he chose to stay in his card game rather than go to his wife because he was afraid of responsibility, and he thought that his wife would not miss him. The effect of that choice was that his wife died alone. Then the gambler chose to run away rather than face his father-in-law. The effect of that was that he lost his family, his dignity, and eventually, his life.

"If you do not take the opportunity to observe yourself, as in the case of the gambler, then you will not realize that your life is filled with choices. The gambler could not realize that he was creating his own life and, in fact, felt like a victim to his wife and her family. In the female life that we will view now, you did not believe that you had a choice until after your physical death. Therefore, you died a victim and saw your own darkness only in another."

Shature was feeling tired now, but she knew that it was really denial and, yes, fear. Facing her darkness was much more difficult than appearing as someone's Angel. As she entered the dome, she braced herself for what she believed would be her greatest challenge yet.

* * *

Ancient Egypt

This time, Shature found herself experiencing the story as a participant rather than as an observer. She was not too happy about this since she knew that something happened in this life that pulled her into her dark side. She began to feel a panic arise from deep within her and she knew that she would have to calm herself in order to remain detached. Yes, something very bad *had* happened. She could feel the evil overtake her like a million spiders crawling on her flesh.

"You are feeling the Black Magic around you," spoke the Guide in response to Shature's thoughts. "You are now in a life in ancient Egypt, and you are a Priestess of the Temple of Set. The Temple of Set brought the teachings of the Dark Robes to Egypt at the fall of Atlantis. The name Set means 'cutter' or 'isolator'. Set's followers seek initiation through self-deification and call upon the forces of isolation and limitation to free them from what they believe is the 'delusion of unity'. They desire the experience of the greatest individuality without any responsibility to others and without the consequence of their actions. They believe that the end is more important than the means. They achieve the fulfillment of their desires through the use of Black Magic, which is the interaction with the disharmonious energies of the third, and lower fourth dimension.

"Do you remember how you feared and avoided the Dark Robes on Atlantis? Your Soul could not understand their Black Magic. Your unresolved fear drew you into this life so that you could learn why one would choose to follow the darkness rather than the light."

"Yes," whispered Shature, as if she were trying not to disturb the forces of darkness that clung to her. "I can feel that I am totally selfish. Nothing is more important than my own self-advancement, and anyone who might assist me in that purpose is disposable once I am finished with them. I can feel that I am ruthless, cold, and completely without love. How will my fifth dimensional consciousness ever assist one who has no ability to love?"

"I am here with you," said the voice of the Guide. "I know that it is difficult for you to experience this life as a participant. However, your lessons are advancing and you are ready for greater and greater challenges. Keep talking to me with your mind. It will help you maintain a link to your consciousness as Shature."

Shature was glad to obey the Guide's request. Perhaps if she could talk about what she was experiencing, it would help calm her fear.

"I am a woman of about twenty five years," she began. "I sense that my name is Nubnoset which means, 'servant of Set'. I am standing in front of a man with a high hat and dark robe. He has a long black mustache that extends past his chin and outlines a mouth that is firm and strong. His eyes are riveting. I cannot lower my gaze to encompass his body. All I can see is his stern, dark face and a huge hat decorated with rubies and emeralds."

"Who is this man?" asked the Guide to keep Shature aware of her higher consciousness.

"I can sense that he is a High Priest of the Temple of Set. He is my lover...No... he is my father. NO...he is both! It is acceptable in this culture for a man to take his daughter to bed. We have been lovers for many years, and we have a daughter named Nephrite who is thirteen years of age. My father doesn't want me anymore. I am too old, or rather, our daughter is 'old enough'.

"I am begging with him not to embarrass me. How can he cast me aside? I am telling him that since I was a young girl I have served him and his evil God, that I have done unspeakable things to myself and to others because he asked me to.'"

"'HA,' he laughs at me. "You chose to serve 'my' God and were happy to do so as long as you felt the power.'"

"His words cut me like a knife. How can that be true? How could I have actually enjoyed a life so filled with selfish and depraved deeds. I look into the heart of Nubnoset and shudder to realize that he has spoken the truth. I have used others to achieve my own ends and pushed them aside when I was satiated. I have ruined my life for a man who has never cared for me. I am not even sad that I may lose him. For the first time since my initiation into the Priesthood of Set, I am afraid. I am afraid that I will suffer for what I have done to others.

"I fall to the ground in a plea for mercy. I hold onto his ankles and tell him all that I will do for him if he will just not cast me aside. He laughs again and kicks me away. I kneel on the ground at his feet and cover my face with my hands as I sob hysterically.

"'Will you die for me?' he asks as he kneels down and lays his dagger on the floor beside me. He pulls my hands from my face and smiles his sinister smile as he looks into my tear-filled eyes.

"For a moment, time stands still. I am looking into his face as he smiles at me, almost lovingly. But he loves only himself. What can I give him? I can give him my death like others have given their deaths to me. He picks up the dagger and offers it to me. I know the dagger. He uses it for sacrifices to Set.

"I stare into the glisten of its sharp, curved blade for what seems like eternity. All the times that I used that dagger on others flashes before my eyes. Yes, of course, in the end I will use it on myself. I am to be his sacrifice now. I take the dagger, and he chuckles as he stands and walks across the room where he will watch me die—for him.

"I place the point of the blade just below my sternum. I know how to make the kill quick and clean. I learned it from him."

* * *

Then, all went black for a moment as Shature fought to remember who she was. She was not Nubnoset, but Nubnoset was a portion of her. However, there was also a life on Venus, her Guide, and Lamire. Yes, she must think of her life upon fifth dimensional Venus in order to rescue herself from the depths of Nubnoset's Hell. Shature took a slow, deep breath and realized that she had detached from Nubnoset, who was lying at her feet. She looked around, and, with a cold chill, she realized that she and the etheric form of Nubnoset were in the lower Astral Plane.

Shature remembered how she had feared this plane while she was in Atlantis and Faerie.

Everywhere she looked was a blood red darkness that was almost black. She heard wails and cries in the distance, but all she could see through the heavy and sticky blackness was herself and Nubnoset. Nubnoset gradually aroused and slowly sat up. Although Shature was touching her, Nubnoset was aware only of herself and the hatred that she held inside of her for the man whom she blamed for causing her death. She must seek revenge. Shature tried to communicate with Nubnoset, but was instead swept back into her mind. Shature's Guide called to her.

"Speak to me, Shature, and tell me of your experience."

* * *

From her place in the lower Astral Plane, Nubnoset, with Shature locked in her consciousness, could observe the physical plane where she had just "died".

"He thinks that he can discard me like a slave." Shature heard the thoughts of Nubnoset—her thoughts as Nubnoset. "I will not have it. He will be sorry for what he has done to me. I will use my physic powers to influence someone to poison him. Xaria, his servant, is beginning to hate him for what he has done to her. I know that I can influence her to put the poison in his goblet."

Shature tried to be the observer and connect with the mind of Nubnoset, but it was impossible. It was only with feelings of compassion or love that Nubnoset could recognize Shature's call, and Nubnoset had neither. Shature was trying to understand how her Soul could have chosen such a life. What could she have learned? She died just as cruelly as she had lived. As she sank back into Nubnoset's consciousness, Shature heard the voice of her Guide reminding her to continue speaking to him.

"I have done it," spoke Nubnoset as she observed the physical plane. The consciousness of Shature was trapped within Nubnoset's bitter thoughts and words. "Xaria hates the High Priest very much. I have spoken to her in her sleep and used my psychic influence, plus a little Black Magic, to give her the idea of putting poison into his goblet. There he is! He is going to drink from the cup.

"But wait. He is pausing. Could he suspect? He always knew when someone was against him. Could he know that it is I? He is looking at me as if he can see my ghost! He is smiling as he sets down the goblet and leaves the room. I hear him in the other room talking to our daughter. He is telling her that she is so special that he will allow her to drink from his cup.

"He knows! He knows what I have planned to do. He can see me even though I am dead and he is sending our daughter to her death just to spite me.

"I watch in horror as Nephrite enters the room and walks toward the poisoned drink. What can I do? Who can I call to help me? My daughter cannot see me. Since my death, I have come to her many times in her sleep and have tried to tell her about the High Priest, but she will not hear. She loves him like I did when I was young, before the evil overtook my heart and robbed me of the ability to love. She is as foolish as I was and will meet the same end.

"I must call someone. I cannot call on the forces of Set, as they are the cause of this. I must call on the other side. I must call upon the Light. But could the light hear my voice? I have turned to the darkness and become as wicked as my father. I have totally given my Soul over to the forces of darkness in the name of what? It certainly was not Love.

* * *

Shature pulled herself from the trap of Nubnoset's consciousness and saw a small ray of light enter the darkness of their Hell. This was her chance. Nubnoset did love someone. She loved her daughter and was trying to turn towards the light to save her. Maybe now Shature could maintain an observer-consciousness long enough to serve as Nubnoset's guide. Shature pulled the Violet Fire around her and tried to remember her childhood as Nubnoset. Had she ever believed in Spirit? She then remembered Nubnoset as a young woman sitting upon her mother's deathbed. Nubnoset's mother had believed in the Violet Fire and had given her a cartouche with the name of Archangel Zadkiel engraved upon it in hieroglyphics. Her mother had told her that the Archangel Zadkiel was the guardian of the Violet Fire and that she should call upon him for protection. Shature whispered to Nubnoset to remember her mother.

Suddenly, the name Zadkiel came into Nubnoset's mind and she seemed to awaken to her bleak environment for the first time.

"Where am I?" she asked Shature, whom she could now see.

"You are dead, Nubnoset, and you are in the lower Astral Plane. Some have called this place Hell."

"Yes, I have come here at my death because of the corrupt life that I have lived."

"And," continued Shature, "because you have wished ill upon the living. But you have remembered love-- love for your daughter, and have called upon the forces of Light to assist you in saving her. I am Shature, and I am here to answer your call. Do you remember Archangel Zadkiel?"

"Zadkiel, yes, The Order of Zadkiel, and the Temple of the Violet Fire. I had a small cartouche that my mother gave me at her death. She told me that it had been passed down from mother to child since the time of Atlantis. I was to hold it and call to the images with my mind when I was afraid. But I knew my father wouldn't approve. I loved him more than my mother, so I put the cartouche away in my drawer and soon forgot it. Do you think that I could call to it now after serving the darkness for most of my life?"

"It is never too late to remember the light," comforted Shature.

"But I no longer have a voice. I no longer have a body. And I fear that I no longer have a Soul. I gave them all away because I wanted my

father to love me. Do I care now for his love? He has forsaken me even after my death. Now I must save my daughter or she shall meet the same fate. All I care for is the life of my child. I must call upon the Violet Fire. But how?"

"Do you remember how your mother called the Violet Fire? She tried to teach you."

"But I wouldn't listen," continued Nubnoset. "It was something about consecration of every portion of yourself. I cannot remember now, and I must hurry to save my daughter."

"Nubnoset," Shature spoke gently. "There is no hurry because you are no longer bound by Earth time."

"Yes," spoke Nubnoset in a moment of sadness. "I am dead. I have wasted my life by giving it to another. I will not allow my daughter to waste hers. I cannot!"

"Then say the words of consecration with me. I will help you," spoke Shature.

"Beloved Archangel Zadkiel, I call upon you to consecrate me in the Forces of Light."

Nubnoset repeated the words and then her dark eyes registered light.

"I remember, I remember the dedication. I will say it with you."

Together, they finished the decree.

"I consecrate the energies of my life stream as it flows from the heart of the Sun!

"I consecrate my physical body, my emotional body, my mental body, and my etheric body to the service of the Violet Fire!

"I consecrate my eyes to see only the Light.

"I consecrate my ears to hear only the sound of the One and the still small voice of the Presence!

"I consecrate my mouth to speak only with the tongues of Angels!

"I consecrate my mind that it may receive the clear and direct consciousness of the Higher Self.

"I consecrate my hands that they may heal and my feet that they may walk upon the Path of Light.

"Take this form, every cell and atom, and consecrate it to the service of the Light.

> "Blaze, Blaze, Blaze the Violet Fire!
> transmuting ALL shadow into
> LIGHT, LIGHT, LIGHT!"

All was still.

They watched the physical plane below where Nephrite paused as if she had heard the decree. Then the room began to shake, and the table holding the goblet tipped and the goblet fell to the floor, spilling the contents.

The Light had saved her!

But wait! Nephrite was dabbing up the poisoned wine with the hem of her gown and touching it to her lips.

"NO! NO! NO!" called Nubnoset. "Archangel Zadkiel, you must stop her!"

"She will not die," resonated the powerful and melodious voice of Zadkiel.

A ray of Violet Light streaked through the darkness as Zadkiel spoke. But when the light faded, the blackness returned and Shature was again pulled inside the consciousness of Nubnoset. The distant voice of her Guide was the only thread of light that connected Shature to her fifth dimensional self.

"Speak to me," he called to her.

"I am still in the lower Astral Plane," spoke Shature from deep within the consciousness of Nubnoset. "It has been three Earth days since my daughter touched the poisoned liquid to her lips. I fear that she will die after all. No, she has died! Here she is. She can see me now."

"'No, Mother, I am not yet dead, but I linger so close to death that I can now see your form. I must know. How did I get so ill? Is it from the wine? Were you trying to kill me, as Father has said?"

"No, my daughter, I tried to poison him, but his will was too strong. Why would I poison you with his goblet? Somehow he knew my plan and sent you to drink from his cup to punish me. I do not condone what I have done. I wanted to murder him because I could not face my own darkness. I had to blame my evil choices on him. But all of my actions were my own. Please, dear daughter, do not make the same mistakes that I did.

"I called upon the forces of the Light to assist you when you went to drink from the goblet. That is why the room shook and the goblet fell to the ground. Archangel Zadkiel has told me that you will not die. I must believe his words. The faith that I could not have for myself I vow to have for you.

"Dear Nephrite, I beg you. Do not allow him to corrupt you. My mother tried to warn me, just as I am warning you, but I would not listen to her. When you awaken, and I know you will, go to the top drawer of my red dresser. Inside there is a

small cartouche that my mother gave to me. Wear it, my dear, and it will protect you."

The image of her daughter began to fade because her body was calling her back. Nephrite would not die.

*"You will have the strength, my daughter, that I did not," Nubnoset called to Nephrite's fading form. "You **will** be able to say no to him."*

* * *

The last vision of Nephrite was gone, and Nubnoset was left alone in the lower Astral Plane. Even her connection to Shature was forgotten. Shature had gone so deeply into Nubnoset's consciousness to assist her with saving Nephrite that Shature had become lost in the caverns of Nubnoset's tortured mind. Nubnoset heard a voice calling from deep within her unconscious, "Shature, Shature!" but she did not recognize the voice or the name. The darkness of her environment had separated her from her Higher Self. Nubnoset was alone. She was abandoned to the darkness in her death, just as she had been in her life. Abandonment, yes, that is what her father had threatened over and over again to coerce her into doing his will. Now, finally, she had stood up to him from the other side of the grave.

A memory came to her of how her father had locked her in a small, dark room until she had agreed to do anything just so that he would release her. The total darkness of the small, foul-smelling room had always terrified her. Every time she was locked inside the room she tried to confront her fear and relax into the darkness, but it reminded her of the wicked things that were done to her and that she had done to others. She realized now that it was not just the fear that had made her beg him to release her. It was the guilt and shame as well.

Now, once again, Nubnoset was in darkness. Her greatest fears in life had become her reality in death. Was this to be her punishment for the evil life that she had lived? Was she to exist eternally alone in the deepest darkness? Alone, with only her fear and shame to remind her of what she had done. Unlike the dark room of her childhood, there were no walls here -- only an infinity of nothingness. But she had made her choices. Her mother had not followed her father's ways. It had cost her mother her health, but at least she had her Soul. Nubnoset knew that she deserved this death to atone for all the suffering she had caused in her life.

But wait-- was that a small glimmer of light off to her right? No, it was merely her imagination. Then she heard a voice. It was the same voice who had called the name Shature earlier.

"If you can imagine the Light, then you can choose it."

Nubnoset did not understand the meaning of these words, but they did prompt her to look to the light again. It seemed somewhat brighter, but it flickered on and off with the surges of fear that engulfed her. In fact, there appeared to be a connection. When she gave into her fear, the light grew dim or and even disappeared completely. When she summoned the courage to face her fear and the deep guilt and shame beneath it, the light grew brighter. The fear seemed to control the Light.

She wondered if, inversely, the Light could control the fear. If she chose to focus only on the light, would the fear diminish? Deep in her mind there was a warm chuckle from the unknown voice. The warmth of the voice amplified the light, which made it easier to find in the clawing darkness. She focused on the light more intently now and found that as she did so, the fear faded. Could she choose to see only the light? Could the light distract her from her fear and anger—anger at her father and anger at herself? Yes, she was angry with herself. She knew now that she had always blamed herself for giving into her father. But, could she have stopped him? No, she had been a child. She had no strength against her powerful father. Had there been a small speck of light inside that room, or inside herself that she could not see because she was afraid? But, of course, she was afraid. How could she judge herself for that? She had been a child, and she was no match for her father. He had manipulated her with the dark room and with his dark mind. He always knew just what to say and how to say it so that she would believe him. He even made her believe that her mother did not love her and that he was the only parent who cared for her!

Nubnoset knew that she would have to forgive that child and forgive herself for giving into the power of her father. With that thought, she felt a warm glow arise within her ethereal body. The glow felt almost like love, but she wasn't sure. She had not had much experience with love. She felt love from her mother when she had given her the cartouche, and she had felt it from her daughter/sister when she was born. She had never felt it from a man. She had felt only fear and hatred from them. No—wait—somewhere deep in her memory a flash ignited. A face appeared in her mind, the long forgotten face of a young man.

Deep sadness and regret filled her as she envisioned him. Her ghostly form shivered with agony and regret. He was the only man who had ever loved her. She had forgotten him because the sorrow and guilt of his memory were too great. He had tried to save her, but her father had found out about them. She remembered the scene as she relived it. She was only fifteen years old. Her lover was one of the young soldiers who were assigned to guard the halls of the temple where her mother lived. Her mother was still alive then, although she was always ill. Some said it was because of her father's Black Magic.

Nubnoset relived how she had met her young man while he was guarding her mother's door and how they had taken the risk of looking into each other's eyes. Normally, the guards were like statues and were never noticed. However, as she passed him, she felt a pull so strong that she could not resist turning her head. He looked familiar even though she knew that she had never seen him. In fact, as she relived the moment, she realized that he had "felt" familiar. As she looked into his eyes, she felt a pull at her heart and she heard the name, Lamire. But, as she learned later, that was not his name, nor was it anyone that he knew. But now the name alone brought such a glow to her heart that the dim light before her beamed stronger and stronger.

"Shature, Shature!" she heard again in her mind. The name still meant nothing to her. The only thing that was familiar was the "feel" of her one true love and the name—Lamire. She had never known what had happened to her lover. Her father had found them where they secretly met in the garden. She was taken away from him and put in her dark room until she begged to be released. Nubnoset hoped they had simply killed him and not used him for their evil purposes. She knew that her father could make him call for death, beg for death. It was the vision of what they might be doing to him that haunted her as she was trapped in the darkness.

"Release him and I will be your servant," she begged.

But her father knew better than to allow her to make a decision based on love. He left her in her deepest fear and guilt until she forgot her lover—forgot Love! She never knew how long she had been locked away. When finally they released her, she was taken into deep caves of the Temple of Set where the light of day had never shown.

She must return to those caves again for within them was hidden her Soul—but how?

"Follow the Light," she heard the voice that had been calling for someone named Shature. It was now becoming familiar. She looked towards the light and as she did so, she saw that it was moving away from her.

"No," she cried. "Do not leave me." She moved towards the speck of light and it grew stronger, but still it moved away from her.

"Am I being abandoned again?" she cried. The light dimmed as she allowed the old fear to come forward.

"I choose the Light," she called. "Do not leave me. I will not allow the darkness to overtake me again."

The light grew stronger in response to her words and began to move more swiftly.

"The Light is not leaving you. It is guiding you," spoke the voice.

The Light grew brighter and brighter as she followed it, but it was always just beyond her reach. Then she saw a cave. But wait-- the cave was the Cave of Set where she had practiced Black Magic and much worse. The light stopped just within its entrance beckoning her to join it.

"I can't go in there again. It is filled with darkness. However, as she spoke, the light grew brighter and sent a tentacle of itself into the mouth of the cave. It wanted her to enter the cave, to enter her fears and her own darkness that was hidden there.

"I do not want to blame my darkness on another!" she spoke to the impersonal light. "I will no longer blame my father for my own behavior. I could have resisted him like my mother did. In the end, I died just as she did."

"You needed to learn about your own darkness," spoke the familiar voice that now seemed to be inside of her. This voice seemed to be guiding her. Had she known it before?

"You must now learn to view that darkness not as an enemy with whom you must do battle, but as a component of yourself that is always present in the lower worlds. Light and dark are not just 'good' and 'bad' as they are experienced in the lower worlds."

The voice was clear now. Yes, she had known it before-- but when? She certainly had not known it in her life as Nubnoset. The voice continued and disrupted Nubnoset's thoughts.

"Darkness and light are only opposite extremes on a spectrum. Light represents unity and darkness represents separation. If you deny your darkness to know only your light, you allow one portion of yourself to become 'unconscious' to your total awareness."

"I have definitely not denied my darkness. Now I wish to know my light."

"Then you must take this light into the cave and unify it with your darkness."

"Will that heal the life I have just lived?'

"It will help."

"Then, I **will** enter the cave. I don't ever want to have another life like the one I just experienced."

"Yes, that is a wise decision," spoke the voice. "However, it is a dangerous one. Once you have gone deep into your own darkness, you can easily forget your light. That is what happened in the life that you have just lived. You must first surround yourself with the light that awaits you at the entrance to the cave. It is your own light that you felt when you remembered your lover. When you step down into the caves of your psyche, take with you an amethyst crystal in your right hand and a clear crystal in your left hand." A crystal materialized in each hand. "These crystals will protect you and help you hold your light during your journey. Also, use the Violet Fire in the manner that you used it to save your daughter. Remember that your only true enemy is the enemy within that you are not aware of. With your crystals and the Violet Fire, begin your journey NOW."

Nubnoset stepped warily into the dark regions of the cave. She tenaciously held the crystals and constantly chanted for the protection of the Violet Fire. The cave was in total darkness, and the only light was her own. At the entrance of the cave she had felt strong enough to make this journey, but now fear was eroding her courage. She could not see where she was going or where she had been. She was a small island of light lost in the deepest recesses of darkness. Then memories came to her mind-- memories of lives other than the one she had just left. Lives in which she had done to others what her father had done to her. She had kept these lives as a secret from herself to avoid the shame and guilt that they held, and she had created dungeons in her mind to hold them. Now Nubnoset saw the threshold to this dungeon mirrored before her. On the other side of that threshold she knew was every life which she had just remembered, every life that she had just felt. Nubnoset sank back in horror, her light dimmed.

"Shature, Shature," called the voice that had been guiding her. Who was Shature and why was the voice calling for her? Had she know this voice before? Was it calling her Shature?

"Yes," replied the voice. "It is you I call. YOU are Shature."

"No," she argued, "I am Nubnoset, or at least I was Nubnoset."

But she was not sure who she was now. Since entering the cave, she realized that she had been many people in many different lifetimes. Perhaps she had once been the person called Shature. No, wait, she remembered now. Shature had been the name of the one who had helped her save her daughter. And the voice, yes, it was familiar as well. A brief picture crossed her mind of a circular room with a domed ceiling.

"Shature," the voice called again.

Yes, it felt like her name. The voice felt loving, and so did the circular room. She wanted to trust the voice and believe that somehow it was the voice of the wise woman who had helped her. Since she had had so many lives filled with darkness, and then she must have also had lives in which she developed her light. But how could she be Nubnoset and also be Shature at the same time?

"I am a higher vibration of you," spoke Shature who was freed from the depths of

Nubnoset's unconsciousness by her Guide's call and by Nubnoset's awareness of her. "I have come into you from another dimension so that I may guide you. The voice you have heard is *my* Guide."

Deep within her heart Nubnoset felt Shature's love, but her shame of the life she had just lived did not allow her to accept that love.

"I know that it is difficult for you to feel your Higher Self when you have just left a life so filled with darkness," continued Shature in a gentle, caring voice. "Because you had been so alone you forgot that there was guidance upon which you could depend. You could not believe that someone cared for you. From my efforts to assist you, even I became lost in you--just as you were lost. But because you remembered love and followed the light, I have awakened in you. Now I can assist you in balancing darkness with light.

"Feel me within you as we enter the dungeon. Allow my power, my wisdom and my love to be yours. My words will speak through you."

Nubnoset did not understand all that Shature told her, but she could feel wisdom, power and love inside of her that was never present before. Bravely, she stepped across the threshold of her dungeon and saw rows of cells on either side of a long hallway. The scent of decay was nauseating. The vision of horror made her want to shield her eyes, and the sounds of agony threatened to dim her light. She clung to the feeling of this other, wiser portion of herself. Nubnoset held the crystals firmly in her hands, called upon the Violet Fire, and entered the first cell.

Within this cell was a Wizard who had created a monster, simply because he could. He wanted to test his power of creation, and, since he believed he was separate from all life, it did not occur to him that this monster might prey on others. In the end, it preyed upon him and caused his death. The monster and its creator had been locked in mortal combat ever since. Nubnoset shone the Violet Light into the cell. She walked through the bars, knowing that they were just an illusion. The monster and the wizard turned and, for one brief moment, ceased their endless battle.

"Who are you?" they asked together.

"I am the sum total of all that I have been," spoke Shature through the astral form of Nubnoset. "I have come here now to claim you as a portion of myself."

"Why would we wish to join you?" they sneered.

"You have no choice. I am you and you are me. I now step into you and embrace you with my Light. I neither judge you, nor fear you. When I was a child, I spoke as a child and acted as a child. NOW I am of the ONE, and I embrace the children of my Soul.

"The Light of my total Self now fills this cell!"

With these words, the monster and the Wizard were transformed into pure creation and creator.

Nubnoset, with Shature as her inner guide then moved through each cell shining the Violet Fire and embracing the darkness with the light. There was a Priestess of the Darkness from ancient India and an evil witch in early England. There were vicious warriors who cared only for the blood of others, and glory for themselves, and cruel, brutal men who turned their women into slaves to be used for their service and pleasure. There were manipulative women who pulled men into their web like a black widow spider and used their seductive power to harm others.

All of these, and more, were absorbed in the Light.

Down and down the rows of cells walked Nubnoset, with Shature radiating from within her, until all the cells were absorbed and transmuted by the light. The dungeon was empty now and Nubnoset had to transform it as well.

"I must now clear this dungeon with my Light," Shature and Nubnoset now spoke as one voice. "I must own this dungeon as my own. As I stand in the center of this dungeon of my Soul, I NOW forgive myself. I was learning to be a creator and I created separation and limitation. I then abandoned my creations and sent them to their prisons deep within. I NOW am beyond the time and space of separation and I NOW stand in the center of this dungeon and project my light into each crevice and corner to clear all the density of fear, greed and selfishness.

"I shall return, again and again, to transmute the accumulation of my own secret darkness and absorb it into my Light.

*"Blaze, Blaze, Blaze the Violet Fire
Transmuting ALL shadow into*

LIGHT, LIGHT, LIGHT!"

Nubnoset stepped from the cave and took one last look at the life she had left. Below her Nephrite was opening the top drawer of the red dresser and pulling out a cartouche made of a metal she had never seen. She held it by its long chain up to a ray of early morning light that entered a room once filled with darkness. A violet flash flickered before the girl's eyes and danced across her face. Nephrite smiled and pulled the chain over her head. The cartouche hid beneath her gown and rested upon her heart. The room was suddenly filled with brightness. Had more sun entered the room, or was that the light of Nubnoset's daughter?

* * *

Shature lay in the darkened dome for a long time. She no longer feared the darkness. In fact, now she saw it as the shadow side of her light. Being Nubnoset had taught her that. Her heart was filled with love for Nubnoset and her daughter Nephrite. This love came from forgiveness and understanding of her total self. Shature realized now that as Nubnoset she had fallen into the very darkness she had so harshly judged on Atlantis.

"That which we judge, we must one day become, for how else will we understand it?" spoke Shature's Guide.

Shature lowered her chair from the dome and solemnly looked directly into his deep blue eyes.

"You saved me when I was lost. How can I ever thank you?"

The Guide waved off Shature's thanks and helped her from her chair.

"You may thank me best by sharing your experiences with Lamire. He awaits you on the cliffs."

Lamire, the sound of his name filled her heart. "It was also the memory of his love that saved me while I was trapped in Nubnoset," Shature remembered.

"Just as it was the loss of his love that broke your will," added the Guide.

"My will—what does that mean on the third dimension? Even after viewing all of these lives, I do not understand the relationship between my Spirit and my Will."

"That shall be your lesson when your return. Go now. Lamire awaits," said the Guide as he led Shature out the door.

Once outside, the sweet smell of the floating gardens surrounded her. Yes, her Complement awaited her. She could feel his presence like a magnet. She allowed that magnet to pull her to him. It had been difficult looking at her dark side. She realized now that she needed comfort and support.

And, most of all, she needed love.

PART TWO

INITIATIONS

I AM

I AM the mother of your Heart
and the father of your Soul.

I AM the presence of Light
for which you have hungered
your entire incarnation.

I AM the Hope which you seek
and the Promise which you fear.

I AM the Perfection which is calling
and the Caution which holds you still.

I AM your fingers, your toes
your breath and your heart.

I AM all that you have ever been
and all that you shall ever be.

I AM that I AM and
I AM now entering your Body.

Welcome me as a mother
welcomes her first born.

Embrace me as a lover
who has been away and has just returned.

Hold my thoughts ever in your Mind
and the feeling of my essence ever in your Heart.

Know me -- as I AM you now.
Love me -- as I have always loved you.

Yes, I AM the One.
The One whom you have always sought.

I AM in you, over you
around you, and through you.

I AM that I AM and
I AM
ALL THAT IS.

CHAPTER SEVEN

THE VORTEX

The sun was high in the Venusian sky. Shature floated towards the cliffs overlooking the pink sand and the Waters of Light. She could feel that Lamire was waiting there for her. They both had been studying in the Violet Temple and learning how to be the Higher Guidance to their physical embodiments on Earth. Shature now held all of her consciousness in her fifth dimensional, Venusian body. Her visits to her third dimensional Earth realities had been challenging, and she was joyous to know that Lamire, her Divine Complement and other polarity of her androgynous self, was awaiting her.

Lamira could feel the cool pulsation of the Waters of Light as she approached the cliffs overlooking their special cove. She took a long moment to take in the panoramic view of her beloved Home. In her Venusian light body, she could see around her with a 360-degree vision. Behind her was the Violet Temple high atop the Red Mountain. Many of her dear friends were entering and leaving through the Temple's golden doors.

The floating gardens surrounding the Temple were filled with beautiful flowers. These flowers radiated fifth dimensional colors that were not known in the lower dimensions. They also had intelligence, as did all life in the fifth dimension. Fairies and other small creatures lived in the garden. All of this life telepathically communicated with each other and with Lamira. Off to her right was the radiant multicolored glow of the Crystal City and to her left were the evergreen forests and small villages where the Venusians lived when they were not visiting the Crystal City.

Deep love and contentment filled Lamira as she looked at the Venusian landscape. In the Earth lives she had just viewed, she had felt a deep loneliness that she now understood was a longing for her true, fifth dimensional self. Lamira reflected on her third dimensional embodiments that she had been assisting. In some of them, she had been a woman, and in others, she had been a man. However, the pattern of loneliness and lost love was continuous through them all.

Francesca, a Gypsy maiden in medieval Italy, had longed for a Nature she could merge with, like the one on Venus. She had also craved a love like the one that Lamira now shared with Lamire. Illiana, a brave warrior in the French Underground during WWII, had also sought the love, as well as the freedom, that Lamira now felt. Little did either of them know that their own Complement, Lamire, had also been embodied with them. However, the turmoil of their lives inhibited their ability to fully embrace the love that had been right in front of them.

Lamira had also assisted in lives where she had chosen selfish power, even at the expense of love. Lamire had tried to assist her in those lives, but she had turned aside all love from others, as well as from her Self. Lamira needed to communicate with Lamire about these lives. She wondered if there were any Earth lives where she had been able to know, and embrace, the love of her Divine Complement.

Lamira peeked over the cliff that was now directly before her and saw Lamire waiting for her on the warm sands below. Though his eyes were closed and he seemed to be in trance, he felt her presence and telepathically sent her his love. Lamira smiled but paused just a moment before she floated down to him. She had spent so much "time" on Earth that she had to remind herself that on the fifth dimension, she could float as gracefully as a feather. She could also fly great distances if she chose to.

She could also will herself to her desired location and be there instantly by focusing her intention on that experience and surrendering to its pull. Lamira smiled remembering how hard she had had to work for whatever she had wanted in her third dimensional lives. On fifth dimensional Venus, she instantly created any experience, object, or location that she desired.

The warm emanations from the Waters of Light embraced her. Now she desired nothing except to be in Lamire's arms. Lamira leaned forward over the cliff and allowed the emanations from the Waters of Light to carry her to the shore where Lamire now stood, arms open. Lamira knew she needed to merge with Lamire to heal the old scars that had been opened by her visits to the third dimension.

"Yes, I remember that life," said Lamire as he tightly held Lamira to him. She shook in his embrace. She had just told him about her life as the Priestess of Set. Nubnoset, the name she had in that incarnation, had been the lover and partner in evil magic with her father, the High Priest of Set. "I remember when I first saw you," Lamire continued. "I was serving as a guard at the door of your mother's quarters. You were so young and innocent then. I could have saved you if I had defeated your father, but his influence was vast and he was not about to lose you as his accomplice; at least not until it was his choice."

Lamira had not realized how traumatic facing her darkness had been until she was safely in the arms of her Beloved. She looked at him as he spoke, afraid to ask him what had happened to him that day in ancient Egypt when her father captured him. He read the look in her eyes.

"Oh, my dear, you must have been so worried. I escaped, or at least, I escaped long enough for there to be a battle and for them to kill me. I am sure your father was enraged that he didn't have the chance to torture me. But I was a man obsessed. I had to return to save you. It was a gallant flight, and it took all five of his men to stop me. I think I killed four of them, but the fifth one killed me. I died feeling that I had failed in rescuing my one true love. I had abandoned you again!"

Lamira was relieved to know that he had not suffered.

"But, you were courageous," she said, trying to comfort him.

"Perhaps, but still I could not save you. I was courageous on Atlantis as well. I think that my Soul has accumulated a belief: *Guilt is more powerful than courage*."

"That belief is called an engram. My Guide was telling me about that. It seems that certain patterns, especially those that were started in one's first third dimensional life, can become imprinted on the Soul and are repeated lifetime after lifetime."

"Yes, I think that my 'engram' of guilt was first established when I could not help you when you entered that child's body on Atlantis."

"I too created an engram on our first earth day. It is: *Men will abandon me*. Therefore, I don't have to feel guilty that I am angry and don't trust them.'"

"I think I understand," continued Lamire. "Because of our old beliefs, when we are incarnated in a female body, we are abandoned; and when we are in a male body, we are the ones to abandon."

"Yes, that is what I have learned in my studies. After all, we are one."

"Lamira, "Lamire said in sudden revelation. "Didn't your Guide say that in your coming incarnation, you would learn to integrate the polarities of masculine and feminine?"

"Yes, why?"

"I am going to find you in that life."

"Do you mean that we will merge?" Lamira replied in growing excitement. "Oh, Lamire, do you think we could merge while on the third dimension?"

"No, I don't think that the blending of polarities into Unity is possible on the third dimension. But your Guide said that in your next incarnation, you would be born in a time frame when the entire planet would be rising into the fourth and fifth dimensions. If that is true, then we will naturally merge into one androgynous being as we enter the fifth dimension."

"And if we can connect with each other before that," Shature continued, "we will expedite the process."

"Do you think it is possible?" asked Lamire.

"I'm not sure. What I have been learning from my Guide is that anything is possible, if we can imagine it. Once we can conceive of something, we can create a reality in which that experience exists."

"The difficulty will be," Lamire added, "to remember who we truly are and to recognize each other. Let us make a pact now. I will work to release my engram of guilt so that I can believe it is possible to use my courage to be one with you."

"And I will release my engram that I can't trust men," Shature added.

"Yes," smiled Lamire, "Then we will meet somewhere in the third or fourth dimension and join our forces to raise our vibration into the fifth dimension and merge into one united being."

"Do you think that we can ask for third dimensional bodies in the same time frame?" asked Lamira.

"I don't know. We have had many lives together before. We will have to ask our Guides."

"Let us merge into one being now. I want the memory of our merging to be strong in my Soul."

In response, Lamire stood, as did Lamira. They faced each other, eye-to-eye and heart to heart. Raising their hands they placed their palms together to create a circular connection from one heart to another. They then stared deep into each other's eyes and felt their frequencies accelerate as they connected their auras into one. They could feel a tingling that started at the tips of their toes and gradually rose through their bodies, joining two halves of a whole into one complete unit. By the time the tingling reached their now joined hearts, they were floating higher and higher in the Venusian atmosphere.

Then there was a flash of light, and they were deep in outer space. Venus was a glowing orb far beneath them, and Lamerius was a speck of light surrounded by many stars. Gradually, one star came closer and closer. They floated towards it. The star became a swirling vortex directly before them, and they were pulled into it. They felt a swirling sensation as the vortex surrounded and transported them. In a burst of light, they were on their home world of sixth dimensional Arcturus preparing for their mission to come to Venus and eventually to Earth. Lamerius had forgotten about their sixth dimensional reality, but now they had returned to it.

It was early dawn upon the planet of Zantrill, and the sun was just rising above the horizon. Since the planet's vibration was of the sixth dimension, it was beyond the polarity of dark and light. However, the inhabitants of this planet, who lived in units of thirty-two, known as pods, had chosen a rhythm of inflow and outflow in preparation for their planned journey to the lower dimensions. They had decided to create these cycles to be like the night and day that they would eventually experience on third dimensional Earth. The pods could use the darkness of night as an inflow cycle to journey to even higher dimensions of their being, and the day light, or outflow cycle, to separate into the thirty two different portions of themselves to ground their higher experiences in their sixth dimensional reality.

IlliaEm, the name used for the planet's group consciousness, oversaw the pods from dimensions above their own. IlliaEm had created the hologram of the planet, the pods, and cycles of day and night. All of the members of the pods would make the journey to Venus. Some would then move on to third dimensional Earth when they had learned to survive in a lower density, and some would stay on fourth and fifth dimensional Venus to act as guides for those who went to Earth.

All thirty-two members of each pod were like the fingers of one hand. Each was individual in the collective consciousness, but unified in awareness and purpose. All were androgynous. In fact, they were beyond the concept of gender, as it is known on the lower dimensions. The portion of IlliaEm that had formed into the pods had chosen to answer the call of Earth and to enter into the great experiment of separation and polarity of third dimensional experience. All those in the pods were of one consciousness, and they would all have the experience of third dimensionality, even if their particular individuality remained on Venus. The adventure was beginning. There was no fear or sadness. These emotions would not be a part of their awareness until they joined the evolution of Earth.

Lamerius felt a harmonic resonance with one of the thirty-two members of the pod. They recognized this to be the higher resonance of themselves. Their body was made of light and looked like a star that a child would draw. They had two radiations that came down from their middle, somewhat like legs; they had two radiations that came out from the middle, somewhat like arms; and they had a glorious crown of radiance that arose from the top, reminiscent of a head. In the middle of their form was a beautiful vortex like the one they had just entered. However, their form was very fluid and mutable and existed only when they desired it. They frequently existed as formless, pure consciousness.

When members of the pod met while in pursuit of their individual endeavors, they would merge into one form as a manner of greeting. They would then return to their individual, yet united, vessels. These vessels were actually only individual if one looked at the brightest portion of their emanations. Upon closer observation, all "individuals" were connected by a dimmer emanation, like a gossamer wing. This wing, or web, was the network that connected all of them and gave them a group consciousness that was beyond imagination on the lower dimensions. Through this network, they were in instant and constant communication with each of the thirty-two members of their pod and with the other pods as well.

While preparing for their departure, they learned that they were not just leaving; they were also staying. They were bi-locating and keeping a portion of their consciousness on Arcturus while sending another portion of their consciousness to fifth dimensional Venus. Since sixth dimensional life was beyond the limits of time and space, this was not impossible. Each pod could easily be at two, in fact, many locations at once. They could travel away for a very long "time" and then return as if they had never left. The only difference was that they had a new experience within their consciousness.

Lamerius was reliving their pod's preparations for the descent into the fifth dimension. The pod went into a group stasis, somewhat like Earth's sleep, and joined together in complete Oneness with IlliaEm. Lamerius felt the pull of the Oneness. If they allowed themselves to enter the unity of that Oneness, could they ever return to Venus and eventually to Earth? In response to their thought, the pod embraced them with their emanation. Lamerius was gone. Arcturus was gone. All form, all thought, all emotion – GONE!

Back on Venus, Lamira and Lamire opened their eyes and dropped their hands. They looked into each other's eyes, their own eyes, and smiled.

CHAPTER EIGHT

THE PRIEST

"The web of unity that you experienced on Arcturus is a higher vibration of the web of light that circles Earth, which you first learned of during the fall of Atlantis," spoke Shature's Guide. Lamira returned to the name Shature when she studied in the Temple because it was the first Earth name she had ever had. Therefore, that name helped her to better associate with her Earth lives.

"Will we use that web of light again when I re-enter the third dimension? It saved Earth during the fall of Atlantis. I am sure that it could also assist in raising the vibratory rate of the planet."

"You are correct, Shature. I am pleased to see that you are learning to pull together all the threads of your various Earth experiences. It is the ability of perceiving all life as a component of the One that will allow you to remember your multidimensional consciousness while on Earth."

"Multidimensional consciousness?"

"Yes, the ability to be conscious of more than one dimension at a time. This is an ability that is very difficult to attain on the third dimension, easier on the fourth dimension, and natural on the fifth dimension. You have been experiencing multidimensional consciousness while in the dome and connecting with your third dimensional realities."

"However, sometimes I become lost in the third dimensional experience. Then I am no longer multidimensional," laughed Shature.

"Yes," smiled the Guide. "The emotions of the physical world activate your fourth dimensional self. On the fourth dimension you can perceive the third dimension, as you did in Faerie, but you lose your awareness of the world around you. Here, on the fifth dimension, you are learning to experience more than one reality in your mind at a time. With practice, you will be able to live as many as seven realities in your consciousness at once. On the sixth dimension, such as Arcturus, you can consciously experience hundreds of realities at once. And, from your Oversoul on the seventh dimension, you can simultaneously experience all your realities into and including the third dimension."

"I have a lot to learn," said Shature shaking her head.

"Oh no, you do not have to learn anything. You have only to remember what you have always known. Just as your fifth dimensional self will continue to exist when you re-enter the physical plane, your higher dimensional selves are infinitely in existence as well."

"Do you mean that my Self as Lamerius will be in existence?"

"Yes, and if you, and Lamire can re-enter your third dimensional realities with the remembrance of Lamerius in the forefront of your consciousness it will be easier for you to recognize each other should you meet."

"Do you think that Lamire and I may be able to meet when we re-enter the third dimension?"

"Anything is possible if you believe it," reminded the Guide. "In the lives that you will observe next, you were able to raise your consciousness and join with your Divine Complement while in your physical body. Are you ready now to observe these lives?"

"Oh, yes. This sounds like it will be much more enjoyable than facing my darkness," Shature replied as she lay down upon the chair and rose up into the dome.

* * *

When Shature entered the dome, she was surprised to see not a holographic picture, but one man standing before her. He appeared to be an Egyptian Priest, but definitely not of the Temple of Set. He was clearly in service to the Light because his aura was a glorious corona of colors and tones, which were known only in the higher dimensions. He was dressed in a simple white robe without adornments. It was difficult to discern his facial features through the glow of his aura, but he appeared to have a beardless face and white hair. Shature could not see his expression, but she could "feel" that it was one of pure love.

The priest stepped forward, and as he did, a flow of recognition entered Shature's soul. He smiled and his entire form expanded.

"Greetings to the portion of my self known as Shature. I am known as Rahotep. That is the name that we took after our great initiation. I have taken on the form of the physical body, which we wore at the time of our embodiment as an Egyptian priest. However, now this portion of our being is no longer limited to a physical shape for we were able to raise our vibration to the seventh dimension upon translation from physical life."

Shature looked confused.

"Do you mean that you are one of my realities?"

"Yes. We are the same soul. I have come to you to tell you of our story to assist you in remembering the completeness of your total Self. I am a portion of you, and you of me. We are of the One. But, let me tell you of a time when I was not aware of this fact."

"Rahotep raised his right arm and pointed to a holographic picture. As the scenes were displayed, he narrated the story of Shature's life as Rahotep.

Ancient Egypt

"When my parents had my birth chart done, they learned that my destiny was not with them, but with the temple. Perhaps that is why I never felt love from them in my earliest years. It wasn't until I entered the temple at five years of age that I experienced the love that a family can offer. I studied and served while I was a child and a young adult. My youth in the temple was filled with loving instructions and wonderful friends. I knew some in the Temple did not share my feelings, but I loved every minute of it. I felt as though I had finally come home.

"In the life that you will be entering, you will face a great initiation. Therefore, I wish to share with you only my Final Initiation, which I started with my first Saturn return at about twenty-eight years of age. My outer teachers told me that they considered me ready to take the Final Initiation. However, I was to wait until I received my inner instructions. I was told to inform them when my inner guide, Radula, instructed that it was TIME. This instruction came a short while after my teachers had given their permission. How many lives had I had to prepare for this moment? A rush of vague pictures from these lives ran past my mind's eye. Deep within me I felt a call of destiny not yet manifest. I was excited and scared.

"I knew that the three possible outcomes from this Initiation were success, insanity, or death. The second two choices were not acceptable to me. Although I was not afraid of death, as I knew it to be only a recess, I felt that I had not yet fulfilled my purpose for incarnation. I did not want all the years of study and work to be for my personal gain alone. Perhaps when my initiations were finished, I would better know what my service was to be.

"At last, the day arrived. The moon was full and I was ready. I had been staying in quarters specially built for those awaiting initiation. From these quarters, it was only a short walk through the desert to the Great Pyramid where every initiate spent seven days and seven nights deep in the bowels of the Pyramid. These seven days and nights were used to review past lives and lessons. If I passed the first portion, I knew there would be more, but the secret of the rest of the initiation was strictly guarded.

"As expected, I had not been able to sleep the night before. At dawn, three hooded priests came to my door just when the first rays of the Sun cleared the horizon. No words were exchanged. The priests led me from my room and into the desert. I had always loved the desert at sunrise and sunset, just when the Sun rose or dropped below the horizon. The horizons in Egypt were infinite—as infinite as Spirit.

"As I followed the priests to the Great Pyramid I reflected on the soft, golden glow of light. As the desert welcomed a new day, I would welcome a new life. I felt a warm anticipation that matched the rapidly approaching heat of the desert. I was at one with all of nature. The vast vistas of my outer world nudged my inner visions to prepare for awakening. The desert was still, as was my mind, and a warm, gentle breeze caressed my face as if to say, "Good luck!"

"I smiled in reply and silently followed the priests as we entered the Pyramid. Although the Sun had been barely above the horizon when the priests and I entered the Great Pyramid, I was unprepared for the total darkness that surrounded us. One of the priests carried a small oil lamp. It was the only thing that I could make out as we moved deeper and deeper into the Great Pyramid. I had learned from my lessons that the total darkness in the pyramid was meant to prepare us to face the darkness inside of ourselves.

"Finally, we arrived at a small wooden door, very simple in design. From the glow of the single lamp, I could see the grains in the wood, a golden latch and a lock hanging open. The priests would lock me in this room for seven days and seven nights – totally alone. They opened the door, led the way inside and instructed me to sit upon a simple papyrus mat on the stone floor. The oil lamp was placed on a ledge to my right along with a small skin of water.

"'This lamp will burn for only three days and nights. After that you will be in total darkness.'

"These were the first words spoken by the priests. They said no more. I heard the door close and, with a soft clicking sound, the latch was locked. I closed my eyes and began to meditate. Within those seven days, I reviewed my lessons of that life and all the others. I went into the land of the dead again and again to give penance for any that I had wronged. I reviewed every lesson that I had ever received in any life that I could access. I don't recall the oil lamp flickering out nor reaching for the water. I only remember the soft click of the latch. This first external sound heard in seven days snapped me back into my physical body.

"As the priests entered the room, I saw their hooded faces over another oil lamp which one of the priests held. I slowly nodded to them to show that I was still alive and cognizant. They nodded ever so slightly in response and motioned for me to join them. It took me a while to stand up, and when I did, I could not walk. I leaned against the wall and willed the life force back into my legs that had been crossed in one position for seven days. The priests took my now empty oil lamp and water-skin from the ledge and waited patiently. When I was able to walk, they led me from the room.

"I didn't know where I was going, but I knew that since I had survived the first part of the initiation, I would be allowed to take the next. The halls within the pyramid were as dark as before, but now my eyes were accustomed to it. The small lamp of my three guides shone like a star for me to follow. The guides walked slowly at first to allow me to get used to my body, but quickened the pace as soon as they knew I could keep up. We moved down, down, and down. I had learned that the Final Initiation room was somewhere deep below the surface of the desert, exactly below the apex of the Great Pyramid. Finally, we came to what appeared to be a dead end as we were facing a stone wall. The priests did not seem dismayed by this turn of events and formed a semi-circle in front of the stone wall. While I stood off to the side waiting for what would happen next, each of the priests began to tone a sound which I thought must surely arise from the core of their Souls.

"At first their toning seemed random. But gradually, a pattern could be discerned until, at last, there was a crescendo of beautiful harmonious tones. As the singing faded into the surrounding darkness, it was replaced with a low rumbling. Gradually, the stone wall began to move to the right. Behind this simple stone barrier was a pair of magnificent and ornately carved golden doors. As more and more of the doors were revealed, I knew that I had seen these doors before in my meditations. One of the priests approached the golden doors and placed one hand on each door. The doors were so well balanced that with just the slightest push, they swung open into a huge room. The priests gestured for me to enter. The doors quickly closed behind me. Again, I heard the low rumbling of the stone wall covering all trace of the sacred initiation room.

"The brilliance of the room blinded me. I had never experienced such illumination while in a physical form. Slowly, slowly, my eyes grew accustomed to the light and I began to survey the room. This room was not of my Egypt. There were domes and pillars studded with lapis, emeralds, rubies, diamonds, amethyst and jewels I could not identify. Colors I had never seen were painted upon the many carvings, statues and figurines that seemed to move as if they were alive. Somehow I knew that everything within the room was very ancient and had a life-force greater than anything I had ever known. This was architecture seen only in my inner journeys to Atlantis.

"The large center dome sheltered a smaller pyramid that was a vibration rather than a physical structure. Anubus and Thoth, the ancient Egyptian Gods of Initiation, stood within the pyramid on either side of a large sarcophagus. The sarcophagus was mounted on a stand of pure gold with silver steps leading up the right hand side. The sarcophagus was made of a substance that I had not seen before. I knew instinctively that this substance was not of this planet and had been given to Earth millennia ago by the first inhabitants of our planet.

"The sarcophagus was ornately carved in the same non-Egyptian manner as the walls around me. I sensed that although the sarcophagus was opaque, it could become translucent if the proper alterations were made by the observer's mind. Anubus motioned for me to enter the sarcophagus and Thoth nodded in agreement. Again, there was no verbal communication. The journey from the doorway to the silver stairs was the longest journey of my life. As I climbed the few stairs I realized that if, indeed, I lived to descend them, I would not be the same person as before.

"I lay down inside the sarcophagus. The substance was hard as stone and yet smooth and warm as skin. I felt as if I were re-entering the womb. The flat, stark walls seemed to slowly mold themselves around my form as I settled into the sarcophagus. I don't think that I could have moved even if I had chosen to. Then Thoth leaned his head over the edge of the sarcophagus and spoke three questions to me in an unknown language. I did not know what the questions were, but I intuitively knew that they were indeed questions and that my survival depended upon my answering them.

"I sent a call to Radula and then, from nowhere, I saw the lid of the sarcophagus slowly enclose me in my tomb. Silently the lid was fastened tight to signify my transition. Again, I was alone.

"If I stayed in the tomb too long I would die. There was little oxygen inside, so if I were to keep my physical self alive, I would have to raise my consciousness to the higher dimensions so that I could feed it with Spirit. I knew that I would not be able to leave my body through my third eye as I had done many times before. I searched inside myself for a portal to use to free my Spirit from the confinement of its physical form. I began to feel a deep fear arise within me, but I willed it away. I must not allow myself to experience an emotion that would drop my consciousness!

"'Where is the portal to your higher self?"

"I now understood the first question. I remembered the chanting of the priests outside the stone door. I could not use my voice, as there was too little oxygen to waste, but I felt the vibration of the toning just as I had with the three priests. Since I was not limited to a human voice I was able to sing all three parts at once. The melody and frequency calmed my fear and raised my consciousness. I found myself concentrating on a doorway inside my head, at the very core of my brain. As I continued to tone, something solid, like the stone door, began to open, and behind it were the very same golden doors I had seen upon entering this room. These doors opened inward. Once again I stepped through them and felt them quickly close behind me. At first I saw nothing but golden light which embraced every cell and atom of my form and consciousness.

"Then slowly, off in the distance, I saw a vortex beginning to form. It began to swirl, slowly at first, and then faster and faster. It was gold, silver, blue, violet, and the other colors that I had first seen in the room outside the sarcophagus. I felt a pull to step into the vortex and with my decision to do so, it was suddenly just before me. I fell into the core of it and found myself spinning faster and faster through timeless space. At first I was dizzy, but then the spin became so intense that I felt totally still, yet at the same time, it felt as if every cell and atom had quickened its vibration in response to the spin. Then, with a pop, my spin stopped and I found myself in the midst of a great void. I had become fifth dimensional and all was calm.

"'Where is the Crystal City?'

"With the second question, there was a golden light before me which became a golden form-- my Divine Complement. She came in the form of a woman since I embodied a man in that life. We embraced in deep reunion and love. She looked into my eyes and whispered, 'I will take you Home now'.

"Then we were on Venus. It spread out before us with all the beauty and harmony that I had remembered from deep within my Soul for all of my lives. My heart opened in a burst of Light and Love that would have exploded my earthen body had I been in my third dimensional consciousness. I saw the mists of Venus all about me. I saw the flora and fauna of my beloved Home as they floated about me in loving welcome. With their every movement, harmonious colors and sounds echoed their motions.

"A welcoming party formed a pathway that led us to the main entrance of the Crystal City. My

Divine Complement slipped into my form as we became One again for our homecoming. Translucent crystal gates swung wide as we approached them and a golden path lighted our way to the heart of the city. The Golden Wisdom Temple was set in glimmering splendor at the end of the path on top of a hill. The doors were open, awaiting our entry. Even though we could have instantly willed ourselves to our destination, we moved in the same swimming/flying motions as those around us because we enjoyed the journey and the community of others.

"Eventually, we found ourselves standing in front of the mighty Sanat Kumara, the planetary Logos for Earth and Regent of Venus. Rami Nuri and Djwhal Khul, as his advisors, stood on either side of him. The Divine Complements of all three flowed within them. They were androgynous. They were complete!

"I bowed before them and Sanat Kumara handed me a jewel. The jewel was unlike anything I had ever known. It was more a vibration than a substance, yet it had beauty and form. I took the jewel in gratitude and held it within my heart.

"My Complement and I spent what seemed a lifetime on Venus. We lived and loved and died. And then I began to feel a pull. I knew that the pull was my destiny. It was Earth. It was calling me to return to my third dimensional life so that I could fulfill my destiny there. I had to return in order for the body to live. The sadness of that realization shook my very Soul, but I remembered my commitment. I had said that I would stay on Earth. Therefore, I had to return, before it was too late.

"The sudden density of the sarcophagus was a shock. How could I have returned so quickly without even a goodbye? And then my heart felt the love of my Home and my Divine Complement. Yes, there was no goodbye, for I would hold them in my consciousness, but what about the sarcophagus? There was even less oxygen and now I was fully physical.

"'How do you open the sarcophagus?'

"The third question was translated in my heart. Yes, in my heart was the answer--the jewel--- the vibration of the jewel. It would raise the lid. And then as I focused my attention upon the jewel within my heart. I heard my first physical sound since the three questions were spoken to me a lifetime ago. The sound was of the lid of the sarcophagus slowly rising. I felt the oxygen rushing to my rescue. Like a newborn infant, I took my first breath and sat up.

"'You are free!' I heard Thoth say in Egyptian, my native tongue.

"After weeks of contemplating my initiation I realized that my lessons now lay in finding the "spiritual" that dwells in the "physical" rather than in the "spiritual" alone. I told my teachers this, and they agreed with my decision. I retired to my small cell to meditate and felt my inner Guide come to me at once.

"'Oh, Beloved Radula, help me. How can I accomplish this part of my destiny?'

"'You are to leave the temple.'

"'No, no! How can I? It will be like leaving home,' I cried.

"'Exactly,' replied my Guide. 'The time comes when even children of the One must leave the safety of home in order to find a new life. Your time is now!'

"I awoke from my meditation with a sense of anxiety. Where was I to go? How was I to unify and ground myself in the physical world? I had learned to unify and surrender myself to the spiritual world, but there had been many teachers to help me. Now I would be alone. On the Spiritual Path, there had been a longing, a call Home. But now, I felt compelled more by duty than by loving and longing, and I knew I must leave the Temple. Life there was too sheltered and my task could not be completed in that environment. The Temple was only partly physical and therefore only partly my place of purpose.

"I suppose I could have stayed there, but it would have taken much longer to accomplish my task of grounding my spirit in matter. As they say in the physical, "time is of the essence." I didn't know how long I could maintain my commitment to a path that was so challenging to me. Even in the holy vibration of the Temple, the low vibration of the third dimension tended to distort the visions of my Initiation. I knew I must take the chance of venturing out into the world while my lessons were still strong in my memory—"the greater the risk, the greater the victory." And, most importantly, I had to follow my inner instructions.

"So with tears in my heart, I said goodbye to all that I had known and loved. I could not hope to make my many friends and companions understand why I had to leave, as I barely understood myself. Only Radula understood. So, without looking back, I left my beloved Temple, perhaps forever. But what did forever mean? Now that I had traveled beyond time, many words had no meaning. How would I ever relate to the people of the world when I could barely relate to the rules of the physical plane? Many questions filled my mind as I left my beloved temple behind me.

"The first six months could have been years or eons. My many activities were too inconsequential to note. The mundane responsibilities of life were unmanageable for me. I had never learned how to care for myself in the world. How to get and prepare food and find a place to sleep was a new experience. All my physical needs had been taken care of in the Temple. Now that I was on my own in a world foreign to my mind, everything became a task and an effort. How was I to desire, much less gain, a sense of unity with a life that I could not even begin to understand?

"Many times I doubted my purpose, as well as my sanity. In fact, many believed I had failed my initiation and had been cast upon the streets instead of leaving of my own free will. They could not understand why I would try this unknown task. A priest was supposed to stay in the Temple. He was not supposed to go out into the streets to help the people. The people were supposed to go to the Temple when they needed help. And, if they could not get to the Temple, they did not get the help. It was the will of the gods, and the people did not question it. In fact, I found that they did not question anything, except whether or not I was insane. I was attempting something that had never been done, and it frightened them. However, on the bright side, I felt an inner knowing that I was following my destiny. Therefore, I continued on my new path.

"Finally, I found a wonderful valley. The energy there was different from anywhere else I had experienced. In this valley I could feel some of the high vibrations that I had known in Temple life, but they were different. Perhaps they were more grounded in the earth, like I was learning to be. I found great joy in wandering the hills near my camp. There was a small pond with a magnificent tree next to it. I spent long hours in meditation under that tree. The energies of the Goddess began to enter into the base of my spine. For the first time in my life, I felt that I was a member of the physical plane. I began to achieve a relationship with Nature that was unknown in the Temple, where we constantly strove to leave our bodies and journey into the other worlds. I was beginning to understand the meaning of my inner directive.

"A few people gathered about me, though neither they nor I understood why. I lived very simply and in harmony with my environment. The people would bring me food and I would heal them or listen to them. Is there a difference between the two? A strange peace was growing within me that felt very much like the peace of the valley. I had spent my life finding a connection to Spirit and now I was discovering a connection to the earth. I found that I was beginning to enjoy it.

"The people who came to me were special. I was close enough to the town that these people knew I had undergone my initiation. They also believed I had failed and had to leave the temple. However, they still came. Therefore, they chose to listen to some inner voice and to ignore the outer voices, which told them I was insane. Some had come out of curiosity and soon left. Most, however, came because of an inner call, and they were the ones who stayed.

"Gradually, people began to bring their sleeping mats or simple tents and camp with me. Our life was very peaceful. We rose at dawn to greet the Sun. Our ceremonies were simple and individual. Each person found a spot and greeted the Sun from that place every dawn. I knew not how they greeted it, as I was busy myself and had chosen not to observe them. If they told me, which they usually did, I listened without comment. When they asked my opinion, I referred them to their inner guidance. I told them all that their inner voice had guided them to me and would continue to guide them. I acted merely as an interpreter. Just as they had been led there, they would eventually be led away. I remained loving, yet detached. I knew that my earthly lesson was to stay detached from any public acclaim. However, I feared that part of my lesson might be to face the challenge of success and adulation.

"We ate what came to us and were as grateful for a meager meal, as we were for a feast. We knew that food was a taste that could corrupt. We were clear not to become attached to it. When the people had learned to heal themselves, they usually desired to learn how to heal others. I was sure that these were extraordinary people who had come to learn and not merely to be healed. Some remembered much of what I taught, and others were unable to retain what they had learned. I remained flexible so that I would not repeat what they already knew or push them too hard to learn new information.

"After a year or two the group had grown to about fifty people. Some came only once in a while, some regularly, and about twenty people lived there. I felt a restlessness beginning to stir within me, but I didn't know what it was. I knew that something was about to change, but I was not sure if it was my body, my environment, or even my consciousness. Unfortunately, I also knew that this change would not be easy, and I would have to warn the twenty who lived with me. I knew that certain members of the town were worried about what we were doing. I needed to be ready to move at any time.

"I finally told the twenty that it was time to leave. I could feel the growing discontentment of the town. Since we lived in such a simple manner, they refused to believe we were of the Light. Gold and jewels surrounded the priests of the Temple. If the gods were on our side, why weren't we provided with material riches? The town members believed that there could not have spiritual powers without riches. Since they were unlikely to possess these riches, they would continue to believe that they had to go to the gods for power as they could never find power by going within themselves.

"Unfortunately, I had stayed too long. Many angry and frightened people came upon us in the night. Four of the twenty were killed, and ten were wounded. The remaining six escaped into the night. The wounded ten and I went into the back lands to heal ourselves. Even though there was much violence, I was unharmed. I knew not why. Perhaps there was still some greater protection at work. I knew that the six who ran away would not return. I felt their disillusionment. Many of those who had not lived with us were also either disillusioned or afraid. A number of loyal friends psychically found our hiding place and brought us food, water, and news of the town. Some of them felt that it was their task to stay in the town and carry on the work in a silent way, and the rest would move on with us when all were healed.

"I discovered how difficult it was to maintain my belief in free will, and accept love, in the face of such adversity. In the Temple, the surroundings and superstitions about the gods and their priests protected us. Here, all of my protection lay within me and I always had to feel it so that I could protect the others. I felt responsible for the deaths and the injuries. If I had acted upon my inner prompting more quickly, I could have averted any injury. This was a hard lesson to learn. I would have to remember to instantly react to my inner guidance. I was not in the Temple, the land of gentle instruction. There might be only one warning, and the consequences could be merciless if one did not heed it.

"Our small community had disturbed the townspeople's sense of reality, and they had retaliated in a frightened, violent way. I had learned the hard way that my work had to be done quietly, away from those who were unable to accept a new reality. I learned that those who could not find comfort in their own beliefs would feel threatened by new ideas. One must first find the core of his/her own truth before embracing another. Old foundations must be uprooted before new ones can be laid. The people who had harmed us were not evil. They were afraid.

"When we began moving, some of the band decided to stay behind. I had spoken to all of them, individually and as a group. Most understood what had happened and were even relieved to know that I was human. However, some were looking for a god-person and could not bear to learn of my frailties. These people would not be coming with us. I had determined to always discuss my human emotions and misgivings with my group. It helped me to understand the human part of myself and it also guarded against adulation from the members of the group. I did not wish to have the burden of being anyone's god. I was merely a teacher and a guide. I understood from my Temple work that humility had not been one of my strong suits in past lives, and I needed to endeavor to hone that virtue.

"After many months of traveling, the numbers in our band had decreased further. Finally, we found a place were we could stay for a while. We had traveled through many barren lands and finally found ourselves in a small, tropical area. There was water and fruit. Also, caravans traveled through this area and would gladly trade their staples for a healing, dried fruit, and whatever other services we could provide. The oasis was quite large and we could be far away from where the caravans filled up their water. Therefore, only those who followed an inner call actually arrived at our camp. Usually, one or two of us would go to the watering area and offer a trade. Several of the group could read auras quite well. They would always go along to see if there was danger. We were getting wiser and more careful.

"After about six months, I sensed it was time to move on again. This time I would not wait too long. The word of our work had spread and many had come especially to be healed or to learn. However, there had been increasing problems with the caravan leaders who feared we were somehow a threat. We had found a valley with water two days' walk away. We could come to the oasis solely to trade while we carried on our other activities at a safe distance. I wondered when the wandering would cease. Were we forever destined to move farther and farther away so as not to offend others?

"The transfer of locations went quite easily. All of us did our part. We could see now that this was a much better spot. There was a small stream that arose from the ground at the top of a low hill and stayed on the surface long enough to form a fair-sized pool before it again became subterranean. One of the women in the group gave birth to a male child. We then had our first natural citizen. Citizen of what, I did not know, but it appeared that some sort of community was beginning to form. I didn't know how new people got there, but they came on a regular basis. Some of them had heard about us from traders and, somehow, the word spread to others. A few came by divine guidance, as they could not remember how they had found us.

"Then one day, a Prince from a faraway land came to us with several of his bodyguards. I had an uncertain feeling about this event. I knew that it would lead to some new development, and I didn't think I would care much for it. However, I was there to follow instructions from within and I was beginning to be at peace with allowing each new development to formulate on its own. The Prince began coming regularly. He had a rare genetic disease that he believed I could cure. He had come to us because of a dream and recognized me instantly. I told him that his karma had dictated this disease to him, and his task was to fulfill this karma. Once his karma was balanced, the disease would be cured. However, I did not know if this cure would come in life or in death. I had grown very fond of the Prince and was having trouble maintaining my objectivity. I had to constantly remind myself to accept the decision of his Soul and not to hold any fear or sadness.

"The Prince and I talked many times. As we looked into his other lives, we found that he had been very hard-hearted and could not see the suffering of others. Therefore, in this life his heart was not of sufficient elasticity. We finally decided that in order to balance his karma, he was to live among his people as a peasant for one year. We felt that if he lived through this, his condition would improve--if he allowed himself to recognize, and be sympathetic to, other's pain. The Prince's father, of course, was not happy about this agreement, but he would do anything to try to heal his son. I was to travel with him as often as I could. This would mean considerable hardship, as the journey was long and dangerous, but I felt I must continue as the path unfolded.

"After almost a year, the Prince was much better. Soon his healing would be complete and he would return to help his father rule. This was none too soon, as the father was very old and ready to leave the physical plane. I tried to prepare the Prince for this possibility, but he was resistant to hearing it. I feared this would be the final, and most difficult test, for the Prince. He had become a very dear man and I was sure he would be a kind and just ruler. I doubted he could attain the wisdom of a Pharaoh, but he would fulfill his destiny to the best of his potential. This was all one could do in any life.

"Finally, the year was completed. The Prince had just returned to his home when his father died. I spoke with his father on the other side and found that he had known all along of his impending death, which was the only reason why he had agreed to my plan. The plan had been very successful. The Prince spoke with his father before he died and was able to face his death bravely. I was happy for the Prince, who was now the King. He had grown from being sick and frightened to a strong and virile man. The new King wished me to begin a temple for him to provide healing and education for his people. I would do so. But as soon as it was started, I would leave some of my most advanced pupils to run it, and then I would move on.

"The King had given me free reign to teach as I wished, and I soon found myself in quite a position of power. He built me a beautiful temple, and there were many priests and priestesses beneath me. I was the High Priest, and there was no one to put me in my place. The schools were successful and the people were remarkably open to my teachings. Many wished to worship me and make me something that I was not. The recognition and praise was more of a threat than a treasure, and I constantly monitored my feelings to note any speck of clinging to earthly prizes. I called constantly to my inner Guide to keep me balanced and to keep my consciousness centered. But, despite my efforts, I began to fear the call of the riches, adulation, and comfort. I feared them because I began to enjoy them--too much.

"There had been no fear in me in the wilderness, but even though I missed the days of solitude in nature, I never left my luxurious temple. In the lap of luxury, fear--and yes, arrogance--began to invade my consciousness. I worked very hard to purify myself, but each day the wealth and recognition altered my mind and hardened my heart and I began to change. I was torn. Should I stay there and continue my work, or should I retreat into the wilderness to save my Soul?

"Before I knew it, it was too late. I began to wear the golden garments and I decorated my quarters like a palace. The food I ate was the best in the kingdom, and I starting looking at women as if they were something to be taken. I knew I could leave, but also knew that I would not. I found it more and more difficult to reach my inner Guide and could not understand what was said when I did. Deep inside me I knew I could not understand their message because I did not want to hear it. Somewhere in my Soul I had always known that my test would be to maintain my purity and humility despite the power, fame and wealth brought by worldly success and recognition. Even though I had suspected such a challenge, I had failed. I lived this way for several decades.

"Then one evening, I had a dream. I dreamed of Radula. The Guide that I had forgotten had somehow gotten through my resistance and touched my consciousness. Standing mutely before me, Radula displayed a scene of an old man dying alone in the desert. I awoke with a start, but could not move. Slowly, my years as a High Priest were reviewed in my mind. And then I remembered my young ideals and ethics. I felt old and tired. How could this have happened? How could I have lost myself to the temptations of the flesh? Were the ways of the world so tempting, or was I just weaker than I suspected?

"I prayed to Radula to return, but there was no response. I was starving among the most delicious of foods and thirsting amongst the finest of wines. My heart was aching when a kingdom loved me, and I was poverty stricken when anything I touched could be mine. The rich foods and fine drinks had weakened me. Many years of using only my mind while others waited upon my body had made me dependent on the comfort and softness of the life I had created for myself. I even had three wives and had fathered five children without being a parent to any of them. How had I lost control of my life in such a way? My anguish was my secret since I had grown dependent upon the worship of others and could not allow anyone to see me vulnerable, even my old friend the King.

"The fine foods sickened me and the drinks nauseated me. The women bored me and the soft environment suffocated me. What was to become of my Soul? I longed to return to the simple days of the wilderness. Perhaps if I returned there I could regain what I had lost. I had grown soft and weak in both body and mind. I was so tormented that I became ill. A fever raged for many days and I suffered the death of the old man alone in the wilderness again and again. Finally, I vowed that if my health returned, I would return to my roots, no matter what. The next day, I awoke, totally cured. My answer had come. I must journey alone into the desert.

"I told no one of my plans. I gave my riches to the poor, except for what was necessary to take care of my children and their mothers. I feared that they hated me because they did not agree with what I thought was 'enough'. But, I couldn't leave them to the corruption of my riches. I feared I still had no love for them, but I wished them well as I left alone at dawn and traveled into the desert.

"After about a week of travel, I found a small oasis and settled in to find myself. At last I felt contentment in my beloved wilderness. The beauty of nature far surpassed the riches of man. Every being in nature spoke to me as an individual. There was no deification or jealousy. I was simply a member of the society of earth. I had left the Temple with only a beast and a few provisions, and soon the food was gone. I had learned as an initiate to go many days without food or water, but now I could not raise my vibration enough. Nor did I wish to. As I traveled alone, I had come to realize that I had gone into the desert to die. It was I who was the old man dying in the wilderness. Gradually, I allowed the life force to leave my body. The hunger that I suffered when my food was gone was one of purification and cleansing, and I felt all the weight of 'success' fall from my body. I let the beast go so that it could find its way home, and I gradually slipped into delirium. I had regained contact with Radula. The love of my Guide was more important than the adulation of an entire kingdom. In just a few more days, I would be spent of the Earth.

"Maybe I had given up or maybe I had followed a divine directive. I would only know for sure on the other side. I could not continue any longer. The vital energy had left my body and now it hovered just above my heart. To some, my life was a great success. To others, it was a complete failure. At that point, I could not tell which was right. I had done the impossible and it had destroyed me. The last two days were as long as my entire life. I had surveyed every moment of it and wished I could return for corrections. However, I was now too weak to get the water that was not far away, and hunger had long since left me. On the seventh day, I left my body completely. As I took my last breath, I already felt lonely for the body that I must leave. I felt great anguish for the end of my life. All I could do was ask forgiveness.

"I called to Radula for forgiveness and understanding. The last thing I saw was the Prince, who was now the King, rushing to save me.

"I opened my eyes thinking that I would see the higher worlds, but instead all I saw was the inside of the sarcophagus.

"'NO!' I screamed. I was very confused and disoriented. Where was I? Was I in a grave, sealed alive to slowly suffocate. I began to lose all control of my emotions and went into a state of panic. I pushed at the lid and hammered on the sides around me, but the more I struggled, the smaller the space became and the less oxygen there was to fill my lungs. I started to cough and rasp for air. I was dying. The box around me became smaller and smaller until I could no longer struggle as their was no space. The lid was inches above my nose. However, the absolute restriction calmed me. I slowed my breathing and tried to remember how I got in this place. However, I could not. My mind was blank and my memory gone. Slowly, something began to grow in my heart -- a feeling. At last, I realized it was a feeling of love. At first it was far, far away and more like a memory than a emotion. When I attached my attention to it, the feeling grew stronger and closer. At last, it emanated from deep within my heart. Yes, it was Love, the most beautiful love that I could ever remember. A voice, clear as a bell and soft as the morning breeze whispered to my Soul. I recognized it before I could understand the words. It was my Divine Complement.

"'It is your initiation, Beloved. You are inside of the sarcophagus and the life that you just lived was an illusion, a portion of your initiation.'"

"Her 'feel' and her words calmed my Soul and, gradually, I began to remember.

"'Beloved,' I spoke in a whisper, 'if you had not come to me, I would have died. In fact, I still may if I don't remember how to raise the lid. But if I die with you, I will be content.'"

"'You needn't die, my One. What you need to do is correct your mistake. Find where you began to make your choices from fear rather than from Love and re-enter the illusion to change your intent.'

"Yes, I mused. When did I forget about Love? When did I change my intention? I went back over the life again and again, becoming increasingly aware of the diminishing oxygen level in the sarcophagus. I realized that I had to go into a meditation and raise my vibration back into the fourth dimension because my third dimensional form could no longer survive in the confines of the sarcophagus. My ego was having a difficult time rising above fear. In response to my thoughts, my Divine Complement began to sing gently into my heart. She sang songs of Venus and of Arcturus, our home before we went to Venus. Yes, I had forgotten Arcturus. I had forgotten the frequency of unconditional love that was the emanation of that reality.

"I began to feel my consciousness raising. I felt my form as pure light and again the trapped, physical form was but a memory. My Complement and I were one again. We were complete and androgynous and traveling into the higher dimensions. We saw the Crystal City of Venus below us, but we continued on. Then, we saw before us a beautiful vortex filled with violet and golden light. The vortex pulled us into it and we were deep in the void beyond the vortex. All was still, completely and blissfully still. We were a small speck of consciousness in a void of raw potential. In this void, there were no emotions and no thoughts. There was no movement and no time. For eternity we stayed floating free in the void.

"Then gradually, off in the recesses of our consciousness came a thought. The thought was followed by a sound, and then by a speck of light. The light became a star and the star became Arcturus. The star was far away deep inside of our consciousness. We felt the love of it and allowed that love to act as a tractor beam to pull us closer and closer to our true Home. The reunion with unconditional love was so intense that it seemed to create an inner explosion that repelled us out of the void, beyond the vortex, past Venus and back into ancient Egypt. I cried out in anguish thinking that I had lost my Divine Complement, but I instantly heard her comforting voice.

"'We are complete, Beloved. I am alive within you, and I will always remind you to remember love."

"Reassured, I took a moment to find where in my vision I had arrived. I focused my attention to clear my inner perception and saw the King standing before me. He had just offered to build a Temple for me so that I might be the High Priest and spiritual leader of his kingdom. It was at that moment that I felt the reactions of fear come into my heart and mind, and my intentions shifted from love to fear. What I had missed before, now resonated deep inside my consciousness. I was afraid--afraid of my own corruption.

"Through all of my teachings and initiations, there had been an engram, a core belief, hiding in my deep unconscious. It said: *'Matter corrupts Spirit.'* I was afraid that recognition and riches would corrupt me. This fear went unnoticed and seeped into my consciousness like a poison. Where once I had felt unity with all life, I began to feel separation and limitation. I became separate from those who built and served in the Temple and limited in my ability to view my greater self. My thinking became polarized into good and bad, light and dark. Gradually, comparison, competition, judgment and jealousy became a portion of my mental life while resentment and anger filled my emotions. I longed for the simple illumination of my life in the wilderness where I had felt united with all life and had allowed my Soul's purpose to unfold before me.

"It was the rejoining with my Divine Complement and our journey Home to Arcturus that allowed me to return to that pivotal moment in my initiation vision and uproot the cause of my demise. I then understood that this vision was a preview of my divine mission, a rehearsal where I could find my hidden enemy—my hidden fear! Where had this engram, held tightly to my consciousness with fear, come from? I knew that I had to find the cause in order to heal it so I looked back upon my childhood.

"When I was a small child and still living with my parents, I saw that they were very poor. My father had great difficulty in finding fulfillment in his life. He had studied to be a scribe, but he lacked the necessary discipline and often found himself without work. He had married beneath his class, as my mother was from a family of farmers. However, it was her diligence and ability to grow food for the family, and even to sell at the marketplace, that provided the only security we had. As a small child, I often heard them argue because, when my father did get work, he took the money and gambled it away.

"When I went to the Temple, I thought that I felt guilty for abandoning my mother to her difficult life. Actually the truth was, I felt guilty because I was happy to leave a home with so much quarreling and so little love. From my parents I learned that lack of material comfort could destroy the spiritual connection of a relationship. I imagined that my mother was actually the nurturing, kind mother I wished she had been, and I blamed my father for robbing me of that mother. I believed that it was his selfish and addictive ways that had ruined my early years.

"When I entered the Temple, I quickly forgot my parents and my unhappy childhood. In all the years in the Temple, I never healed this childhood pain because I had ignored the life I was currently living and, instead, focused on my past lives. Therefore, a weak place began to grow in my consciousness. A place where I had hidden my secret childhood fears that my father cared more for money than for me. This childhood fear then expanded into my hidden adult fear that I cared more for success and adulation than I cared for my Soul. These fears bonded with my thoughts and a powerful engram grew, which unconsciously molded my behavior and my life. Because it was an unconscious fear, it was even stronger, as I could not monitor it. My challenge in my initiation was to find this hidden enemy so that I could disarm it with my love force, but I had forgotten the unconditional love of my higher selves and the power this love held. Gradually, I became lost in my secret fears of corruption.

"My Divine Complement came to me to remind me that my physical body, my matter, was only the grounded portion of my Spirit. What I had to do to heal my earth-bound vessel was to connect it, consciously, to my myriad spiritual vessels. I was not a physical being having a spiritual experience. I was a spiritual being having a physical experience. With that knowledge, I could remember to love my grounded vehicle, love my mother, my father and, most important, love my Spirit.

"As I returned to re-live my vision, I would remember that I was a multi-dimensional being. This time I would maintain the memory of and communication with my higher selves. I would keep continuous connection with my sixth dimensional self in Arcturus, my fifth dimensional self in Venus, and my Divine Complement. I would hold the anchor in the third dimension while she was anchored in the fourth. While I took responsibility for the daily activities of Temple life, she would direct the flow of Spirit as we grounded our fifth dimensional Venusian life in the foundations of the Temple and blessed it with the unconditional love from our Source in Arcturus. With this alignment, fear could not take root in my consciousness. I was now aware of my fear, and I could keep it as a guardian to remind me to stay connected to my higher selves, guard against corruption and surround me with love.

"I heard my Divine Complement's voice, 'Allow the Love from within to meet the Love from without in a joyous union of Spirit into Matter.'

"I smiled inside my heart. Yes, I would allow her love into my physical body. In that way, we could become merged while I still held a third dimensional form. Together we would gestate, nurture, and protect the Temple with unconditional love. My Divine Complement would be kept close in my heart and mind to remind me that I was a multidimensional being. Together we could transcend the separation and limitations of the third dimension. I was ready now.

"'Yes, I will go with you," I spoke to the King. "We will build a Temple for healing and enlightenment so that all who enter may learn that love is stronger than fear and Spirit is alive in all matter!'

"In response, I heard the lid of the sarcophagus begin to raise."

* * *

The picture of ancient times disappeared and all that remained was Rahotep. He walked toward Shature and put out his hand to invite her to leave her chair. She had never left the chair and wondered if she would fall to the floor far below. However, his look was so imploring and his gesture so strong and confident that she decided to trust him and take his invitation.

Yes, she WAS healing now if she could allow herself to trust a man. Rahotep smiled at her with a glimmer in his eye, as if he had heard her thoughts. He held his hand out even further, and she reached forward to take it in hers. When she stood, she found no ground beneath her, but she floated in place. Rahotep stood before her with a look that was so loving that she felt her aura fill the dome. He pulled her to him, and, as he embraced her, they blended into one.

"All that I have learned and all that I have experienced is a portion of our total self," he spoke within her heart. "Remember that the greatest enemy is the one hidden inside. If that fear can be brought to your awareness, it can be loved free. Please, accept now the greatest lesson of my life, of our life:

Love is stronger than fear, and Spirit is alive in all matter!"

When Shature came down from the dome, her Guide had left the room. She thought about searching for him, but realized that he had left her to be alone with her thoughts. She needed to ponder her life as Rahotep so that she could completely integrate his gift. She pulled her feet up under her and closed her eyes to go deep inside herself. She took three deep breaths and brought in Wisdom, Power, and then Love with each breath. With her inner vision she saw before her a house of mirrors, with each mirror representing a different reflection of her self. She saw her own essence in each reflection and called in Lamire to complete that reflection. Gradually, a warm glow came into her heart and radiated until each of her reflections included her Divine Complement.

Some of her reflections were on the third dimension, some on the fourth, some on the fifth, and others on even higher planes. But all were of ONE Spirit. She took another deep breath and, as she exhaled, she saw showers of love falling down from the higher dimensional lives onto the lower dimensional lives. Yes, love was stronger than fear, and Spirit was alive in all her lives.

CHAPTER NINE

THE MEDICINE MAN

"I thought that I was assisting my lower dimensional selves, but Rahotep is of a much higher vibration than me," Shature said to her Guide when he returned to the room. She had remained in her meditative state until she heard a gentle click and knew that her Guide had returned.

"Although Rahotep resonates in a frequency higher than the components of your Self known as Shature, as you have just seen in your meditation, he is not of a vibration higher than your Total Self."

"Yes," mumbled Shature, "the house of mirrors."

"Exactly," smiled the Guide. "From this Violet Temple, you have viewed and healed many of your physical lives. In doing so, you have made it much easier to re-enter the third dimension, because your physical body will be able to carry more light. Just as you assist portions of yourself who vibrate on a lower dimension, your higher dimensional selves assist you.

"In my life as Rahotep, my Divine Complement was assisting me from the higher dimensions."

"Yes, because you were able to raise your consciousness into the fourth dimension, you could hear the call of your Complement and merge with her. Together you were able to rise into the fifth dimension and return Home to Venus."

"The story of Rahotep's life has reminded me to surround my sorrow and fear of my fear of abandonment with love. Love will remind me that I am never alone and therefore I can never be abandoned. I am a portion of the One, a Spirit who has chosen to enter into the experience of the third dimension. In higher dimensions, I am One with my Divine Complement and with all of creation. If I can remember to seek unification with my higher vibrational selves, then I will be able to share their experiences of unity and freedom."

"And, they will be able to share your experiences on the third dimension," added the Guide.

"Yes, just as I have grown by Rahotep's merging with my life, the portions of my physical self that I have seen have grown from merging with me."

"The next portion of yourself you will learn from also raised his awareness to the higher worlds," spoke the Guide. "But I wish you to fill your being with the love and spirit of our beautiful nature here on Venus. Being in Nature will greatly assist you in remembering your multidimensional self when you are on the third dimension. The life you will review when you return was one in which unity with Nature is what allowed you to integrate your spiritual and material worlds."

* * *

After communing with her beloved Venusian Nature, Shature was ready to review the next life. When she entered the domed room, she walked straight toward her chair, but her Guide stopped her.

"You no longer need to go up into the dome. Instead allow your own consciousness to project the hologram. Remember, dear, you are not limited to the portion of yourself standing before me. Close your eyes and allow the vision of sixth dimensional Arcturus to ignite the memory of and connection to your completeness."

Shature closed her eyes and remembered Lamerius, her complete self. As united androgynous beings, they had traveled through the vortex to Arcturus. Shature remembered the lightness of their sixth dimensional star body and could feel the vortex in their heart. The pod was around them and unconditional love filled her awareness. She then heard a beautiful tone that was accompanied by a burst of light so strong that it penetrated her closed eyes. She opened her eyes and she saw before her a Native American Medicine Man. He stood calmly in all his pure and regal splendor. He was magnificent. He wore a beautiful ceremonial costume made of buffalo hide and a huge necklace of bear claws. His hair was in long braids and his face was painted with three red stripes on each cheek and an image of what looked like the sun on his forehead. In one hand he held a rattle, and in the other he held a pipe.

"I am How-ta-shai. I returned to the Oversoul in the seventh dimension at the close of my physical experience. In response to your call, I have joined you via this hologram of your creation."

"How did you know that I was calling," puzzled Shature.

"My One, just as you are observing the vibrations of your self at a lower density, we of the Oversoul are observing you."

"Yes, of course," Shature was beginning to understand. "As much as the life I have now is beyond the conception of my third dimensional self, the life of my Oversoul has been beyond my conception. Before you begin your story, could you tell me more about the Oversoul?"

"Of course, close your eyes again and listen to my words with your heart. Just as you have shined a light on portions of your self, feel the light shining on you. The Oversoul is like a lake nestled in the highest mountain peak. This lake is filled with pristine waters straight from the heavens. Many rivers flow from this lake in all directions, which in turn form other lakes even farther down the mountain. From these lakes flow other tributaries which also have lakes, and so on and so on, until the waters of life have reached the sands of the great oceans. As these waters meet the Mother Ocean, they touch the beings who swim the waters of life and call them to re-enter the streams of their birth and gradually swim up until they are at last home safely in the original pristine lake of their Source."

Shature heard a tinkling of bells and another flash of light caused her to open her eyes and turn her head. It was Rahotep, or rather a hologram of him.

"I, too, resonate within the Oversoul. I have returned to assist you in understanding what How-ta-shai has to say."

He walked over and joined the medicine man. Shature saw before her the projection of two very powerful higher vibrations of her total being. She looked around to find her Guide and discovered that he was, again, gone.

"You are doing fine, my child," she heard inside. "Seek for guidance inside yourself now. Remember, we are together in the Oneness. If ever you want me, all you need do is call me and I will respond."

Shature almost felt sorrow at his loss, but she could not hold the vibration of that emotion in her expanded self. In fact, she was no longer just Shature. She was again Lamerius, because the high vibratory rate of the room instantly called in Lamire.

"Lamire, you are with me again," she smiled.

"I am always with you."

Rahotep and How-ta-shai smiled and said,

"We are all projections of the same Oversoul and we are complete within the Oneness. The portion of us labeled Shature is allowing her consciousness to expand to the conception of more than one reality. You are awakening your multidimensional consciousness."

Shature started to feel proud, and again found that she could not resonate to that feeling either. She realized that she was having the memory of pride just as she was having the memory of being as Shature. She understood what Rahotep and the Medicine Man had said. She now held in her consciousness all the realities that she had reviewed. She was on Atlantis, in Faerie, England just after the fall of Atlantis, 13th century Italy, 20th century Poland, and 19th century England, the United States and ancient Egypt. She was on the shores of the red cliffs of Venus, and she was a star-being on Arcturus. Within the ever-present NOW, she embraced all that she had relived. She felt her form expand until at last she was without form. She was a speck of light within an infinite ocean of radiance.

Slowly, she began to constrict herself and her radiance pulled into itself. She pulsated it out again, and it became stronger and brighter. She experimented with the inflow and outflow of her emanation until she gradually returned to the hologram of Shature. Yes, she too was a hologram. She was a projection of form from the Source, and no matter how many different projections there were, they were all from the same Source. Gradually, her perception returned to the domed room and How-ta-shai standing before her. Rahotep had left his hologram of form and returned to the Oversoul, but she felt his presence within her along with the others. She smiled and How-ta-shai smiled in return. The glint in his eyes showed the radiance of all creation.

How-ta-shai was seated down with his legs crossed and gestured for Shature to do the same. As soon as she sat, a small fire manifested between them and a teepee surrounded them. Shature stared into the fire and waited for How-ta-shai to begin his story.

"I will speak to you first of the death of the part of us once known as How-ta-shai," spoke the Medicine Man. "As I speak to you, close your eyes and see the story as I tell it. Listen to me with your heart and hear my truth. It is the tradition of our people to teach through storytelling, and I wish to share that tradition with you now."

How-ta-shai began to shake his rattle and softly chant while the teepee filled with memories. He pointed to his right and there, on a rough mat, was a withered old man on the verge of starvation.

"This is how I looked at my death. My people were defeated and we were imprisoned inside a white man's fort. We could not see our beloved plains, hunt buffalo, or have our sweats and sacred traditions. We were a conquered people."

How-ta-shai turned his focus from the fire that he was staring into and looked Shature straight in the eyes.

"Do you see the theme of the realities that the Oversoul has chosen for you to view?"

"Yes," responded Shature. "They are societies, or me, in transition and the fear that comes with change."

"Yes, we of the Oneness have focused our collective consciousness into you so that you can be our representative on the third dimension. The Earth that you will re-enter is on the verge of a great transition which will affect that entire multi-dimensional universe. We, the many lives you have viewed, had at one time perceived ourselves as failures. That memory resonated in our collective consciousness. You assisted and healed the realities that had not achieved spiritual awakening. Those of us who had learned to connect with our higher selves while we were incarnated were able to heal ourselves and return to our higher vibration. I tell you now of my own frustration while incarnated so you can see that even failure is a success if we can integrate with Spirit."

"But why have I been chosen to be the representative?" asked Shature "Your reality of Shature in Atlantis represents the initiation of our Oversoul into the limitation and separation of the third dimension. It was also a life in which you connected with the grid of light that surrounds planet Earth. You will be called upon to again consciously connect with this energy grid when you re-enter the third dimension. But allow me now to return to my story. We who have been able to rise above the limitations of the physical world wish to instruct you by sharing our experiences.

"As I have said, we were a conquered people and all of my spiritual strength and insight could do nothing to stop our fate. There was one small victory that I was attempting to achieve. I wanted to make the Bluecoats allow us to pitch our teepees outside of the fort where we could at least see the plains and the rising and setting of the sun. There were only old men, like myself, and women and children left. The few warriors who were alive were injured or imprisoned in the Bluecoat's iron house. If we could achieve just one small victory, then perhaps we could keep our Spirits alive until a better day.

"But let me begin my story at a happier time."

How-ta-shai pointed now to his left and there was a small boy rubbing the sleep from his eye as he arose from his skins.

19th Century United States

"This young boy was born to be a warrior. As soon as he could walk, he remembered wanting to ride a horse. If his mother didn't watch him, he would run off to where the horses were penned and try to walk among them. Remarkably enough, he was never hurt. Many times, he would escape the eyes of the adults who were watching him and run to the horses. Once they realized that he wouldn't get hurt, they let him do so. Perhaps he thought he was a horse instead of a 'two-legged.' Or perhaps he just cherished the horses' power.

"As everyone suspected, he became an excellent horseman, and everyone knew he would be a brave warrior until the most unexpected thing happened. He fell from his horse. In fact, he was sure an invisible force had pushed him. He was thirteen and on his first buffalo hunt. He was feeling like a man, but not acting like one because he thought he was better than the horse; he was the hunter. This pride got him in trouble. He wasn't respecting the horse or the buffalo, and when the horse moved quickly to the left, he moved to the right. He was so caught up in the act of being a 'man' that he behaved like a small boy and forgot his very first lesson. He and the horse were one. And so, in his arrogance, he fell from the horse, right into the path of a raging buffalo.

"Worse yet, he fell onto his shoulder and his right arm lay limp at his side. He grabbed his spear with his left hand and, just as the Spirit had pushed him from the horse, the Spirit led his arm true and struck the buffalo with his spear. The giant animal did not die with one stroke, but he stumbled. This gave the boy time to jump up and run to his horse, which waited for him in spite of the great danger. With his remaining good arm, the boy pulled himself on to the horse's back and rode to safety. The other hunters had witnessed this scene and released the buffalo from life. The young hunter had struck the first blow on a mighty buffalo, and he was a hero. However, he realized, as his spear arm lay limp at his side, that he would never be a warrior.

"His shoulder healed much quicker than his heart. He recovered most of the movement of his arm, but he could not throw a spear or use a bow and arrow. Finally, he learned to use his arm well enough to hunt, but he did not have the strength to go into battle. And so he brooded. His life was over. He was not a warrior. He was barely a man! How could he live with this handicap? He was useless. His life was over before it had a chance to begin. He wandered around supposedly on hunting trips, but he had no heart for hunting. He didn't even enjoy riding his horse. He would have to leave the tribe. He had nothing to give and it was selfish for him to stay. He did not know where to go. He only knew he had to leave.

"One morning, before dawn, he gathered a few things and slipped out of the teepee before anyone else awoke. He headed due west, away from the rising sun, and away from his dreams. He did not know where he was going, or why. He didn't care. For days and days, he walked. He hadn't brought his horse, as a warrior needed it and he had no right to take it with him. After many rising and setting suns, he came into a territory that was new to him. By the end of the second moon cycle, he was lost. Of course, he wasn't lost in the sense that he couldn't go home; but he was lost in that he had no idea where he was or what he would experience next. He was not afraid. Nothing worse could happen to him. Maybe if he could lose his past, he could find a future.

"In the distance, he saw a high cliff and decided he would climb to the top to seek his vision. He buried his provisions at the bottom of the cliff, as he would need no food or comfort, and began his climb. The way to the top was very steep, with loose gravel and little to hold on to. After nearly falling several times, and wishing he had a man's strength in both of his arms, he finally reached the top of the cliff as the last rays of the sun were setting below the horizon. He found a small niche in which to sit and curled himself up to wait. The night grew colder and colder, yet he hardly noticed. He vowed that he would not move until he had received his vision. With every hour, he drew deeper and deeper into himself. By dawn, he was in a deep trance.

"Gradually, a storm began to gather about him. It seemed to echo the storm that raged within his soul. The weather became colder and colder, and the wind grew icy. He knew that soon it would be the first snow. It had been many moons since his injury. The plains and the pain of his wasted life seemed far below him now. From his perch on the cliff, he felt like he was a part of the growing force of Nature, and less and less a part of his physical body.

"As the wind whipped about him, he could feel his Spirit being tugged by it. He wished to fly like the wind and roar like the thunder and be free once and for all of the limitations of his wounded body. His anger and disappointment filled his heart and mind, and he wished to leave the clay prison of his body.

"'Grandfather,'" he cried to the howling wind. "Take me with you!"

He surrendered to the pull of nature's storm, and, with a flash of lightning, he was pulled out of his body. He looked down and saw a small empty form clinging to the side of a cliff and could vaguely remember it was he. He took to the wind like a bird. His Spirit knew no limits, and the turbulence in the air only added to his excitement. He didn't know where he was or where he was going. He didn't care if he ever returned to that small shell. He was Home now. He was the wind and the sky that held it. He was lifted higher and higher away from where, and whom, he once was. He seemed to lose consciousness for a moment, and when he awoke, he found himself on the plains. He was alone except for one buffalo that was as white as snow.

"'They are coming to kill us!' it said. 'They will gain power over you by killing us and there is nothing we can do to stop them.'

"With these words, the buffalo turned and walked away. The Spirit of the Indian ran after him with many questions.

"'Who are 'THEY'? Why do they want power over us? How can they kill you?' "But the buffalo was just an animal now. It was no longer white, and it was all alone. The man turned around and saw many mounds off in the distance. He could not make them out, so he went closer to investigate. As he got closer, he saw that the mounds were dead buffalo--thousands of them, lying dead on the prairie. Some were skinned, but the precious meat was left to spoil in the sun. Some were wounded and left to suffer and die a slow death. Some were calves and some were pregnant cows. What was this atrocity?

"Who could do such a thing, and why? The white buffalo's words echoed in his head, 'They will gain power over you by killing us.'

"He must stop the slaughter. He could not allow this to happen. He must return to his tribe and warn them. He could not abandon his people in their time of need. With that thought, he was suddenly aware of himself way below his Spirit, pressed against the side of a cliff. He looked as dead as the buffalo on the plains. His face was white, his lips were blue, and there was snow all around him. He must get back into his body before it was too late. He struggled to return, but the very wind that had given him freedom was now causing his death. The currents of air were strong and they pushed him away from his body. He knew that in order to return to it he would have to WANT to live. He would have to fight for the right to be alive--alive with a purpose. He must return and help his people.

"Gradually, he could feel himself moving towards his body. He reached for it as if he could pull himself back into it. When he finally touched it, it was ice cold. It was too late. He was already dead. If he entered his body now, maybe he would be a ghost, caught forever between two worlds, but he had to take that chance. He had to believe that he could restore himself to health. And then, suddenly, all was dark and he was cold, very, very, cold! He tried to move but could not. His arms and legs were ice, and he could not feel his fingers or toes. He collapsed into a small heap trying to hold within him any heat he could. He had to get warm. Gradually, he found he could crawl. Actually, he was dragging himself with his elbows. There seemed to be an indentation just ahead; perhaps it was a cave.

After what seemed like a very long time, he reached the mouth of the cave. He rolled into it, but it was slanted down and he felt himself rolling out of control. He rolled and rolled until he was suddenly stopped by something big and furry. It was a bear. He didn't care. It was warm. He fell into the warmth of its fur and passed out.

"He didn't know how long he was unconscious, but when he awoke he was warm, or at least he wasn't cold. And he could move. His hands and legs obeyed his command, but his fingers and toes were on fire as though a million bees were stinging him. Rubbing his hands together, he willed himself to sit up and get his bearings. Gradually, as his eyes grew accustomed to the darkness, he found he was alone. But on the floor beside him was a pile of roots. They were almost frozen, but they were edible. Why was this pile of roots in the cave? He knew he hadn't put them there. He still was not sure where he was or how he had gotten there. Then he remembered the vision and his struggle to return to his frozen body, his fall into the cave, and the bear. He had never heard of a bear taking food into his cave. But it was food, and he was starving. He began to eat the roots, and once he started, there was not another thought until he had eaten them all. When he finished, he was thirsty and he crawled to the mouth of the cave, amazed at how weak he still was, to eat some snow.

"Where was the bear? Had he found another cave, or was he on his last search for food before his hibernation? If that were the case, he needed to leave before the bear returned. But with the thought of leaving the sheltered cave, he realized he was still too weak. If the bear were going to kill him, he would already have done so. Besides, he surely could not yet survive outside. He crawled back to the deepest depths of the cave and fell asleep.

"Several times he came to the edges of wakefulness and remembered a large furry lump leaning against his sleeping form. He felt safe, secure, and warm and drifted back into the depth of sleep. When he awoke fully, he often found more roots, which he ate with a great appetite. Sometimes the bear was there, and sometimes he was not. Finally, after an indeterminate length of time, the man was able to stay awake long enough to ponder his situation. This time when he awoke, he found the bear deeply asleep in the farthest depths of the cave. It was almost as if the bear knew that the young man was well now, and so he went into his winter's sleep. The man realized that the bear had brought him the roots, kept him warm, and in fact, saved his life. This was a powerful omen as to the purpose of his life. Nature had saved him and he must pay her back. He had been granted Bear Medicine, and he would learn to use it.

"For two winters he lived in that cave with the bear. How he survived the first winter, he was not sure. When he had regained enough strength, he had crawled down to the base of the hill and uncovered his supplies from beneath a pile of snow. He slept a great deal, snuggled up against the warmth of the bear. Somehow he survived on the supplies he had recovered and the small animals he caught outside the cave.

"His first teachings were in the dream-state. He met nightly with the Great Spirit and received many instructions. Upon awaking, he would walk in the snow to try to anchor these instructions into his physical form. It was during these daily walks that he learned to connect with Nature in a way that he had never done before. All of Nature was asleep, like him, in the depths of winter, but the Great Spirit never sleep and became a constant companion for the man.

"The person that he had always known as he was now dead, and he had not yet given birth to his new self. He was pregnant with himself. He was gestating a new essence from deep, deep inside, which was fed every night in his dream state. As spring began to dawn, so did the seedlings of his new self. The bear awoke and left him alone in the cave. He was surprised at how lonely he felt. He, too, would leave the cave to build himself a shelter against the face of the cliff he had climbed that fateful day at the very beginning of winter.

"As he saw the new life of spring all around him, he began to build a new life within himself. His new self was totally at one with all of Nature. Like his horses, he could smell water, and, no matter how far he walked from his shelter, he could always return. He ate much like his friend the bear: fish from the rivers and a nearby lake, berries, roots, and small creatures.

"One day, while he was eating berries, he felt a strange metamorphosis take over his body. Suddenly, his hands became very large and furry and his back took on an unfamiliar curve. His sense of smell was so intense that he was almost dizzy. He fell down on all fours and began running through the woods at an incredible speed. He wondered if he just felt like a bear or if someone outside of himself would actually see him as one. And then he smelled the most magnificent smell he had ever experienced, a female bear. He came upon her slowly from an upwind direction. But she was too smart for him, and turned to face him. She sniffed the air as if she were confused by his scent. He stood on his hind legs, raised his paws, and growled to impress her. She had no cub and would be ready soon to mate. The man/bear turned and ran up the hill, leaving her awaiting his return.

"He awoke at the edge of a stream beside the berry patch. He was naked and what clothes he had were torn from him and lay in shreds around him. How could he have had the strength to tear his clothes from himself without a knife? Had it been true? Had he been a bear, or was it only a vision? Did it matter? He lived in two worlds now, the Spirit World and the Land of his Fathers. He could travel back and forth and never realize that he had changed realities. Had he lost his mind, or merely exchanged it for his Spirit?

"While he was a bear, he had seen some mushrooms. He would pick them and save them for the full moon, which was coming within a few days. He realized that there was something important that he must do. Grandfather Sky and Grandmother Earth were calling him. He fasted for three days and stayed as naked as he had been when he awoke by the stream. Then it was time. The moon was full and high in the sky. He blessed the mushrooms in each of the four directions, presented them to the Great Spirit, and slowly ate them. Nausea overtook him briefly, but he did not purge himself. He laid back and stared into the moon. She seemed to be speaking to him.

"'Remember. Remember, my warrior?'

"Remember what? he wondered. And a warrior! Was she taunting him? He knew he could never be a warrior.

"'Oh, but there are many kinds of warriors,' she said. 'They are different only in their choice of weapons.'

"'I cannot yield a weapon. Even as a bear, my one arm was weaker!'

"The voice ignored his complaint.

"'Your weapon shall be your medicine!'

"'I have no medicine,' he argued.

"'If you remember who you are, you shall have your medicine. If the bear recognized you, why do you not recognize yourself?'

"'But who will be my teacher? I am alone in the wilderness.'

"'Yes, you are right. The wilderness shall be your teacher.'

"And then the voice stopped and he saw many visions. He saw men in blue clothing with saddles and fire sticks like the trappers used. There were many of them – too many.

"Then he saw fires, and women and children running in panic. The men were gone. Where were they? How could they have abandoned their families? No, they had not abandoned them. He saw the warriors awaiting the battle, but the men in blue were afraid of them, and only fought the women and children. Had these enemies no honor?

"Then he saw naked trees. The leaves were gone, and the trees were tied together to trap something inside. He had to free what was trapped inside. He beat upon the wood, looking for a way in, when he heard laughter. He looked above him and saw a man in blue inside the strand of trees, with his head and shoulders looking over the dead trees, and down at him. The man laughed and laughed.

"'NO!' he cried. 'I do not want this vision. It is evil!'

"The voice returned. 'Cycles end, like the changing moon. But like the moon always returns, so will the People!'

"The next vision he saw, he could not understand. There were his people, only there was no space around them. There were no plains. There were no buffalo. Their warriors lay around like sick old men, leaning up against trees and drinking firewater. They seemed to live in teepees that were not the shape of the medicine wheel, but were flat with something shining on the top. There were things around them that looked almost like the iron horses, but they were smaller and appeared to be broken.

"Everyone was sad and beaten. And then it happened. With a bang of the old wooden door, someone came out of a flat teepee. He was a warrior in full dress. He had his paint and war bonnet on. He carried his best bow and arrow. He did not want the white man's fire stick. And in his other hand, held high, was something bright. Something almost burning, but it did not burn. It was as light as the sun and spread over the entire camp. One by one, the lazy, sick men arose and were transformed into mighty warriors. The chief raised both of his arms high into the sky and summoned the Spirit World. He looked into the warrior's face, and in that one face, he saw the faces of his People.

"Then all went black. He saw nothing more. He tried to bring it back. He wanted to remember everything, but he couldn't stay awake. Something was pulling at his Spirit. The last thing he saw was his naked form lying on the forest floor.

"When he awoke, the sun was high. He crawled to the stream and rolled into it. He lay there for most of the day, crawling in and out of the water, until finally he had to find food. What could his vision have meant?

"How could the wilderness teach him his medicine?

"He spent the rest of the summer answering that question. The vision was still a mystery, but the wilderness was his teacher. The sky taught him how to be free. The birds let him use their eyes to see land far below them. The trees told him where to find roots and other edibles. The bees found him honey, and all the creatures spoke to him in a language without words. As he moved through the woods, he somehow knew that this bark could heal pain and this flower would ease the fire in a wound. Nature gave her secrets to him. As the days shortened and the nights grew cold, his lessons continued. Then he knew it was time to return to the female bear. Did they really mate or was it a vision? All he could remember was that they appeared to become one being. Was she really a bear or was she his Spirit Guide?

"Then winter was upon him and he knew that he would hibernate like the bear. He had gathered his food and an old stag had given his life up for him. His bear mate had told him where to find it. From this gift of Nature, he made his winter clothes and set up his provisions. When he went to the cave for his winter's rest, the bear was waiting for him. He looked at his two-legged roommate and ambled to the back of the cave.

"The man seldom took walks this winter. He was too busy dreaming. He walked the skies with the Grandfathers and returned to Grandmother Earth only to eat and relieve himself. When spring came, he was ready. He didn't know for what, but he was ready. One day he awoke and the bear was gone. He knew that he, too, must now leave the safety of the cave. He gathered his few possessions, as he knew that he would not return. He had received his lessons. He had learned his Medicine. Now he must use it for the good of his people. He would return to them now. He had something to share with them. He was a warrior and his weapon was his Medicine.

"He decided to take one last tour of the valley to say goodbye and to gather provisions for his long journey home. Every tree and blade of grass seemed to know him. The flowers turned in his direction, and the animals, insects, and birds seemed to recognize him. Finally, with the sadness of goodbye and the joy of hope and purpose, he turned one last time as he reached the edge of the valley. What was that he saw in the distance? Yes, it was his bear mate. And beside her was a small cub.

"But what did the vision mean?" asked Shature.

How-ta-shai's face grew gray and sad.

"The vision was the Truth, although it took me many years to know it."

He motioned his hand to the right of him, toward the old, dying man. An Indian woman was entering the teepee with a small bowl of food and a skin of water. The old man waved it away.

"'I will not eat until the Bluecoats allow us to place our teepees outside the walls of this fort.'

"The young woman nodded with sadness and respect and backed out of the teepee with the untouched food. She looked over to the Commander of the fort who was just entering his quarters, set the food down in front of the teepee, and left.

"The Commander had no taste for this job. What was the point in torturing these people further? Every morning, as he entered his office, they placed the old Medicine Man's food outside his teepee. And every evening, they took that same full plate of food away as the commander left his office. He had heard that each remaining member of the tribe had sacrificed a small portion of their nearly inedible food as a gesture of support for their one remaining warrior. The commander had served in the Civil War and had fought many brave battles, but he saw no purpose in shaming these poor, defeated people any more. However, his orders were to keep them within the confines of the fort. Where would they go now? There were so few of them left. The warriors were dead or in prison. But he had to obey his orders, didn't he?

"And then one morning, as he walked up the stairs to his office, he turned to look at the familiar scene of the food in front of the old man's teepee. But instead, he saw the women taking down the teepee and wrapping the old Medicine Man in a burial skin. They all turned to look straight into the face of the Commander, their eyes shown with pride and love. Even the children stopped to make sure he knew what had happened.

"The Commander had seen many terrible things in his long military career, but the simple sight of the loss of one courageous old man struck his heart. He found that he had to lean against the pillar of the porch to regain his composure. He then called his Lieutenant and said in his most powerful voice:

"'Lieutenant, tell these people to set up their teepees outside the fort!'"

* * *

As the Medicine Man finished his story, Shature felt the deep sorrow of "The People." She had heard the story with her heart and was in awe of How-ta-shai's courage. Could she be such a brave warrior when she returned to Earth?

"There are many ways to be a warrior," spoke How-ta-shai. "Remember my story. I had to lose my ability to be a warrior in the way that I had wanted order to be a warrior in the manner that was my destiny. I did not share with you the many years in which I was of great service to my people. These were years filled with happiness, service and love. Later, I had to learn to keep that love alive during years and years of pain, suffering and loss.

"At my death, the only thing that I had left was Love itself. Love for something greater than the material world. Love for an ideal. I had sacrificed myself as a symbol of the love I held for the ways of my people. It took a lifetime of service to achieve it, but I can now give

you a love that is transpersonal and beyond human emotions. This love is an energy field and a beam of power. Take this gift from me and hold it in your heart."

The Medicine Man stood up and Shature followed his example. He circled the fire and embraced her, heart to heart. She could feel his bear energy, his love of Nature, and all his pain that he had transformed into wisdom. Yes, she would hold this gift forever, beyond all life and death, within her Heart.

SUZANNE LIE, PH.D.

THE INNER GODDESS

The Inner Goddess
peers from behind
the Tree of Life
which floats above
the Waters of Emotion.

She adorns Her hair with
leaves which are the
symbol of reincarnation.

Just as the tree survives
the long winter without its leaves,
the Soul survives the
transition of Life to Death
to Life….

Her eyes beckon you
to join Her vibration.

Her heart opens to
receive and express
the Spiritual Essence
which flows from the Source.

Her voice is sweet and clear

and resonates from deep
within your Soul.

"Join me--
My vibration is yours,
My life is yours.

Together we are One
Together we can express

The purity and peace
of Soul's Purpose."

CHAPTER TEN

THE PRIESTESS OF DELPHI

After How-ta-shai returned to his natural formless state, Shature felt a need to be in nature and left the domed room to go outside into her beloved, floating gardens. Though these gardens were vastly different from the woods of How-ta-shai's initiation, they brought about the same sense of unity with all life. Shature's heart, beaming with How-ta-shai's deep transpersonal love, attracted the flowers around her to come and share her joy. Shature blessed each plant that came to her and received its blessing in return.

"I must remember this love and unity when I return to the third dimension," Shature thought to herself. "I know that being in nature will help me in that remembering. When I was How-ta-shai, I gained my medicine by being in nature. I even merged with my Divine Complement through the form of a bear."

Thinking of Lamire made Shature instinctively look towards the pink shores. The bluish hued sun was low in the yellow sky, and she could hear the melodious tone of the waters of light as they caressed the pink shores that lay in the small cove at the base of the red cliffs. The waters seemed to call to her. Shature decided to take her favorite walk to the shore. She wanted to experience each portion of the beautiful landscape around her, so she slowly floated to the shores rather than instantly willing herself there.

Off in the distance, she saw what appeared to be a patio jutting out over the cliffs. Her curiosity peaked. She willed herself there and found that it was a patio made of a type of marble found on Earth. The patio was semicircular in shape with benches lining the outside walls. A shallow pool in the center filled with clear aquamarine liquid glistened with the gold and silver tint of fifth dimensional colors.

Shature thought the scene seemed incongruous. The marble of the patio was of Earth. Yet the cliffs that supported the patio and the colors of the liquid in the pool were of Venus. She went to the pool, bowed down, and put her fingers into strange liquid to see if it was like the water of Earth or like the liquid light of Venus. It was cool to her touch. It felt like Earth's water, but made lovely tinkling noises as she disturbed it, just like the liquid light on Venus.

"It is an integration," spoke a clear and lovely voice from behind her.

Shature turned towards the voice. She saw an elegant woman wearing a flowing, opalescent gown that wrapped loosely around her body and was clasped at her left shoulder with a silver Owl. Her delicate facial features were highlighted by her abundant dark hair, which she wore swept up on top of her head. Small ringlets caressed her cheeks and the nape of her neck. An aura of feminine power surrounded this woman and seemed to radiate from her like a beacon. She wore jewelry that appeared to be made of copper in the shape of snakes on each of her upper arms. Around her neck was a magnificent amethyst necklace with one huge amethyst jewel which hung from the center of the necklace and rested between her breasts. The gem seemed to magnify the radiance flowing from her heart. What struck Shature the most were the woman's eyes. They were as violet as the jewel against her heart and they penetrated Shature's very Soul.

"I AM Matia, a Priestess of ancient Delphi," announced the woman.

As the Priestess spoke, a blur of various pictures rushed across Shature's mind. There was a small girl, a dark cave, and a handsome young man. A warm and wonderful smile appeared on Matia's beautiful face. Her eyes glistened as she spoke.

"Do you recognize me?"

"Y..y..yes," stammered Shature, "I think you are another component of my Self, but I don't understand. I am not in the domed room and I did not call you."

"The domed room was merely a prop that you no longer need. You can tap into your higher power without it now," answered Matia. "And you DID call me, with your heart."

"When?" questioned Shature. "No, wait. I know. Was it when I communed with the flowers that I beckoned the Goddess?"

Matia smiled in response and a tinkling of bells accompanied her nodding head.

"And the patio" continued Shature, "is an integration of ancient Greece and Venus because I am becoming integrated."

"And more powerful," added Matia. "Soon you will return to the third dimension to complete your destiny there. I have come to assist you so that, when you are there, you may assist the Goddess."

The light from Matia's eyes temporarily dimmed and a look of almost sadness temporarily crossed her face.

"The Goddess needs us," she continued in a very serious voice.

Upon Matia's words, Shature felt a burst of love and protectiveness for the Goddess. She remembered how Rahotep and How-ta-shai had found peace and enlightenment in nature. She remembered how Francesca had loved walking in the woods and how Illiana and Stephen had felt their only freedom during their adventures in the country. Yes, she had always loved nature and the Goddess who was the guardian of it.

"Come," said Matia as she took Shature by the arm. "Allow my will to transport us."

* * *

Shature relaxed as she felt Matia's firm hold upon her arm. Matia set her intention and instantly they were transported to the entrance of a dark cave. It was overgrown with plants and weeds, and the mouth of the cave was barely visible. But wait, what was that on the ground before it? It was a tribute. Someone had remembered the Goddess.

"Yes," spoke Matia, "The Goddess is awakening now after eons of lying in the shadow of the patriarchal, armed societies of Earth.

Matriarchal—Patriarchal, female—male, the wheel turns. The battle has been waged for millennia. In the time frame that you will re-enter, it will be different. The polarities of male and female will join, but they will no longer battle. Instead, they will join and step into the next dimensions together."

From the depth of the cave, they heard the voice of the Goddess,

"Arise, my ones, do hear my call
The time has come for one and all

To hear my plea, to know my name
I am the Goddess of our Earth plane.

From high above the Earth's vibrations,
There is assistance to save our nations.

Listen now and do not fear
The answers are for those who hear.

And now, my ones, the time is nigh
The Goddess needs you, hear my cry

For those who don't - I cannot save

One is the master or the slave.

*The time has come to pick which side
One can no longer run or hide.*

*The truth is now, the power here
Do you follow love or follow fear?*

*Against my form no longer sin,
For very soon I begin again.*

*I'll clear my surface free of mire
For of greed and hate I tire.*

*Hear my call and join my voice
Arise, my one,*

*NOW
Make this choice.*

I, the Goddess, am as indestructible as I am infinite. I weary of this low vibration and no longer wish to be limited to it.

For eons I have held this vibratory rate, slowly growing denser and denser as my inhabitants have fallen deeper and deeper into their forgetfulness.

Soon, I will raise my Heart to its higher form!

I wish my children to join me, but I cannot wait much longer.

The moment of in-breath is coming! I need all to focus their attention upon their higher vibration.

It is time NOW that you remember who you are and accept the power that comes with the conscious awareness of your true, multidimensional self."

Shature heard the voice of the Mother with all of her heart as she remembered her many lives on Earth where the Goddess was completely forgotten.

"During the time of my Earth life as Matia, the Goddess's power was waning," said Matia. "Come, let us return to the patio and I will recount my story to you."

Shature and Matia set their combined intention upon the patio at the edge of the cliff and they were instantly there. They then sat across from each other on either side of the circular pond. The hard marble benches became as pliable as the chair in the dome when Shature seated herself. She could feel the energy of this place like a magnet against her skin. This had been an important location in her life as Matia. She could vaguely remember sitting here before. There was a man, one who felt very familiar, and children, many of them. Something significant had happened on this patio. Yes, an important decision had been made here—a decision that involved love and loss.

"Matia smiled in response to Shature's thoughts. "I can see that you are beginning to recall that reality. As I tell you my story, be One with it. As you listen—remember. I will begin with my childhood."

Ancient Delphi

"I had been born with the birth-sack across my face and my mother, taking that as an omen, immediately had my fortune read. The diviner said that I would grow up to be a great oracle and that I should be given to the Goddess on my fifth birthday. My mother was also told about a great decision that I would need to make in my twenty-fifth year that would change my life forever. However, my mother died shortly after bringing me to Delphi and never revealed the decision with which I would be faced. My only mother would then be the Goddess. I would have to seek counsel from Her and hope that I would make the right choice.

"When I first came to the caves of Delphi, my job had been to help clean the caves and gather water from the well. In time I earned my superior's trust and was given more and more responsibility. First, I assisted in feeding the many people who came to Delphi to receive a reading by the Oracles, and, eventually, they allowed me to run messages back and forth from the dignitaries to the officials of Delphi. Everything I did was in or near the caves.

"Others may have perceived the caves as being cold and lonely, but to me the darkness of the caves felt warm and reassuring. It had been home and mother to me since I was five. I had a best friend named Zulia. We did everything together. We ate together, slept together, and worked together as often as possible. It was no surprise when we started our menses on the same day. We were thirteen and so happy that we could barely contain ourselves, because we knew that we would be given our rites of passage together as well.

"The High Priestess had been told that two children were dying and that two women were being born. The High Priestess herself blindfolded us and, holding onto the golden cord around her waist, we were led to the sacred pools deep inside the caves. Only the High Priestess knew where they were. The secret was passed on from one High Priestess to the next. We arrived at the pool exhausted and muddy from stepping in the many puddles and bumping against the damp walls of the cave. For the entire journey we had not been allowed to speak a single word, and if we dropped the golden cord, no one would give it to us. We would have to find it ourselves with our blindfolds still on. Therefore, Zulia and I held on to the cord like life itself.

"At last we were at the pools and were allowed to untie our blindfolds. We were instructed to remove all our clothing and to burn them with the torch that the High Priestess had been holding. She then led each of us to our own pool at opposite ends of the cavern and warned us that we were to have NO communication. Now we would be left alone with only meager rations to eat, and the water in the pool to warm and comfort us. As we stepped into our pools, we found that the water was warm and effervescent. The steam rising from the pools brought warmth to our naked bodies. I found a relatively comfortable ledge by the pool where I would wait and meditate through my first blood. For the first time since we had met as children, Zulia and I could not communicate about our experience. I willed myself to forget about her and to concentrate only on the Goddess.

"'When you have finished your bleeding, call me in your meditations and I will come to birth the new woman and present her to her Sisters,' said the High Priestess.

"Without another word, she took the torch and left us in total darkness. Although, we kept our vow and did not speak to each other, we found great comfort in knowing that we were together. We were like twins awaiting birth from the same womb. I finished my blood several days before Zulia. I went into meditation and silently called the High Priestess. Within a short time she was there. Somehow she had heard my call. I will never forget the joy I felt when the blindfold was removed from my return trip. Now, I was a woman. I was completely changed, but my skin still felt the warm glow of the mineral waters of the pool. My sisters ran to me in welcome. They brushed and styled my hair and adorned me with a long gown with the silver cord around the waist that only the women could wear. My short robe with the rope bindings lay in ashes beside the pools.

"But my joy dimmed because Zulia was not with me. I feared that she would feel abandoned by me and would never quite forgive me. I know I never totally forgave myself. Perhaps I should have waited for her. But I had not. It was a decision I had made and one that I could not change.

"After I was adorned as a woman with my hair atop my head and my long gown, I was blindfolded again and led by all my sister Priestesses. They giggled and chattered like a hundred birds. We were all merry and the anticipation of a great surprise filled the many tunnels that they guided me through. At last they grew silent, and I felt them all watching my response as we went round the final turn. I was still blindfolded and could see nothing, but a warm breeze and a melody of beautiful scents welcomed me. I knew that I was approaching an opening as I felt the light through my blindfold.

"Then all my sisters gathered about me and sang a beautiful song. We called it 'Welcome to Womanhood'. At the end of the final chorus, they became silent and somber. From somewhere in the opening I could smell the High Priestess coming to me. I had learned to recognize her by smell from our journey into and out of the sacred pools. The High Priestess took my hand and led me into sunlight so bright that my face was instantly flushed. She then stood just before me and placed her hands upon my shoulders. I could feel her eyes burrowing into my Soul.

"'Do you swear, Matia, upon your life, to keep the Secret of the Mysteries that are to be revealed to you?'

"'Yes," I replied in a firm voice.

"'Matia," she asked again. "Do you swear to hold until your death the secret of this special place which you are about to see?"

"'Yes, I swear upon my life to carry these secrets into the Elysian Fields of the Netherworld upon my death!"

"The High Priestess embraced me and removed my blindfold. Everyone laughed merrily as I gasped at the vision before me. For many years, I had spent all my sleeping hours and most of my waking hours in or near the cave. Light was something that had been reflective. It reflected off the cliffs near the cave mouth or from the candles and oil lamps. When the blindfold was removed, I was almost blinded by the intense and direct light. But I *could* see, and everywhere I looked was incredible beauty. The Goddess had kissed this valley and hidden it for only her Priestesses to enjoy.

"'This is the Light of the Mother,' whispered the High Priestess. 'If ever you speak of this valley to the uninitiated, you shall extinguish a part of that Light. We keep the Mystery of the Goddess alive within this valley. To go against the Mother is to go against the Secret of Life. If anyone divulges the secret of this valley, they must surrender their lives in repentance.'

"I had vowed with my life to keep the secret, and I meant it. My mother had chosen my life as a Priestess, but I had come to totally embrace it. I had seen the 'kept women' of the dignitaries. They carried their beauty in their jewelry and clothes rather than in their eyes. Their only power was over their servants or slaves. They soon grew fat in overindulgence and shame—shame that they had lost their beauty, shame that their men openly took lovers (male and female), and shame that they had lost themselves because they had lost their connection to the Great Mother.

The price for losing the Mother was too great. I would keep Her secrets, Her power, and Her virginity. I didn't understand what the joy was in sex anyway, at least, not yet.

"I learned later that the cave wound its way beneath a mountain and opened up on a beautiful isolated valley that could only be reached by traveling through the cave or over high peaks. The cave's entrance to the valley had been sealed by a rockslide for unknown years until one of the earliest Priestesses received a vision explaining how to remove the rocks. As the last rocks were cleared, they saw this beautiful, pristine valley. The valley was a secret and only the 'women', those who had passed their first initiation, knew about it.

"The valley was vital in the life of the Priestesses of Delphi because it afforded them the freedom that they needed to do their mission. In the valley they had freedom from intervention, freedom from the outside community and, most importantly, freedom from men--or at least, freedom from male domination. Once, the Goddess had been worshipped by all. They knew Her as the creator of the form of their lands and the form of their bodies. Everyone loved and respected Her and the land that was Her body. All Her subjects were equal. Animals, birds, insects, plants and people were all equal citizens of Her realm.

"But slowly, the Goddess was being forgotten. Times were changing. The men were worshipping their gods of war and possession, and the Goddess held less and less importance to them, as did the women. Women belonged to their men and were for enjoyment and procreation. In fact, one of the few times that the men consulted women was when they came to the Oracle. But would they have listened to these women if they could have slept with them?

"In the olden days, male and female sex was an expression of Spirituality. It was a dedication of their joint energies to the Great Goddess. Men and women would rejoice in the creative force of the Mother and create wonderful magic with their sexuality. But now it had changed. Men used intercourse as a way to possess their women. And women, who were quickly losing their ability to survive on their own without the Light of the Goddess, were using sex to 'trap' men into wanting to take care of them. This is why the Priestesses were virgins. It was not a matter of morality, or purity, or even power, as the men wished to believe. It was because their virginity won them freedom. In the valley, a man's foot had never trod. The women could wander through the many trails in complete nudity, without any fear of judgment or lust.

"After our rite of passage, we were allowed to go deeper into the cave, live in the Priestess' quarters, and serve our older sisters. Zulia was placed in the East Quarters and I was in the West and we were kept very busy with our separate duties. Although we were heartbroken by our separation, we would sneak off to be with each other as often as possible. However, there was something different about our relationship since our initiation. Maybe it was just that we were now women, and before we had been children. One day, while studying together with the High Priestess, she tried to explain this to us.

"'Now you are Priestesses," she said. 'It is not appropriate for a Priestess to become too attached to anyone or anything. Our power comes from our ability to be free of needs and desires, and our freedom is limited if we are attached to the outside world rather than the world inside ourselves. Once, the Priestesses could leave Delphi for two or three seven-year cycles in order to marry or have children. However, in the last hundred years or so, we found that the Priestesses would not return once they left, because the indoctrination of the patriarchal world would erode the memory of their true selves. Many initiates who would have been very powerful Priestesses were lost. Therefore, we have changed our rules. We live in a difficult world now. We women must work together to keep the Light of the Great Mother alive!'

"I did not yet understand the power of her words. I was young and had not been tempted. Zulia had also made her promises and felt much the same as I. We loved the Goddess, and we loved her secrets. More love than that was not needed. Many of the Greek men were fully satisfied by their own sex and openly loved each other when they came to the Oracle. Why couldn't women do the same?

"As I grew older, I took more initiations. I served in the Priestess' Quarters for three more years. Then it was my time to join a group of my sister Priestesses and go into the deepest darkness of the cave to face the darkness within myself. For two years we did not see the light of day. We came out only at night to do our Moon rituals and returned to the depths of the cave to continue our lessons and deep introspection.

"When I was just a child, my life had been so simple. I had had no desire or emotion pulling at my heart because everything I needed was around me. However, at this time I began to have strange yearnings, which I could not understand. I knew that they had something to do with sex, but it was more than just sex, I hoped. It was about love. Suddenly, the love of the Goddess seemed to be lacking in some way, and I needed something that was outside the safe surroundings of my life.

"Not every woman could give up her personal desires for her spiritual destiny. There was the animal body in which her spirit lived which desired to mate and procreate. I understood why the

Priestesses could not marry or bear children in a world were women would lose their power with a man, but I began to resent the limitations of my chosen path. Why must I sacrifice so much for my inner life? Was I not also a woman?

"While deep in the caves, I viewed other lives in which I had had lovers, husbands and children, but still the sacrifice seemed too high. I searched inside my self for an answer and cried to my inner guides for help, but all I found was more pain. When would I ever find peace?

"I was almost ready to resign from the Delphi, when I had a vision, or actually, it was a visitation from my inner guide Pallas Athena, the Goddess of Truth. I knew that it was not an illusion because she touched me. I had been in the cave for two years, had studied past lives, and had faced birth and death many times. I learned the reason I had chosen the parents I had been born to and the reason I chose to incarnate into my present life. I could meditate for many days at a time, without food or water, and I could walk in the total darkness with only the vision of my own inner light. How could I have achieved all of these powers when I still had such doubt and desire locked inside my heart? I felt guilty and ashamed. I felt as though I had been lying to my mentors and fellow initiates. And, worst of all, I as though like I had been lying to the Goddess! I would have to leave Delphi. I did not deserve to stay.

"One day, I could take it no longer and decided to leave that night after all the others were asleep. I did not have to worry about waking up, as I could not go to sleep. At last, everyone was asleep and it was my chance to leave. I knew that I was being a coward to sneak out in the dead of night, but I could not stand another moment of my inner turmoil. Perhaps if I could be alone for a few days, I would be able to return and submit my formal resignation. I rose from my mat and sneaked from the sleeping room like a criminal. Then the most unusual thing happened. I got lost in the mazes of the cave. This was impossible!

"I had lived in these caves for two years and was certain that I knew every inch of them like the back of my hand. I realize now that my Soul had intervened and confused my poor, wounded ego. I was sure at first that I could find my way out of the maze, but instead I seemed to be moving deeper and deeper into unknown territory. At last I realized that I was completely lost. Perhaps this was the labyrinth of the final initiation for which I was obviously not ready. I would die here in this passage and become one of the skeletons that I had bumped into as my flight became more and more desperate.

"Finally, I came to a cavern which I had never seen before. There were stalagmites and stalactites all around the entrance. As I entered, I found that the cavern housed a large pool. Most amazing of all, the cavern was filled with light. It was not direct light like the Sun, but more like the reflective light of the Moon. How could this be? I must be many miles beneath the surface of the earth by now. There could not possibly be an opening to the exterior light at this depth. Nonetheless, the cavern was filled with light. I looked around to find the source of this mysterious glow. It appeared that the light was stronger on the other side of the water. Going around the pool, however, would be very difficult, as both sides rose straight up from the water without even a small ledge upon which to crawl. I would have to go into this unknown body of water in order to find the source of the light.

"I could have chosen to leave the cavern, but since I was totally lost and would probably die anyway, I was daring enough to enter the water. If I died here, at least it would be in an act of courage rather than in an act of cowardice. I entered the water slowly and carefully. My wrap quickly became a hindrance to my movement and

I had to get out of the pool and take it off. I left it by the edge of the water. If I ever returned, I might need it. I now re-entered the water completely naked. The water was exactly my body temperature and felt like liquid skin. It was denser than regular water and completely black. Perhaps it was not water, but some other liquid that I had not encountered before.

"I kept my head out of the water and hugged the edge of the pool, holding on to the small ridge which encircled it. I tried to float my body as close to the surface as possible as I was not brave enough to meet whatever may be living within the depth of the blackness all around me. At last, I reached the other side. I pulled myself from the water, scratching my bare skin on the rough rocks as I did so. I was now naked, bleeding, and quite terrified. However, the light did appear to be brighter on this side and there seemed to be a small path which meandered into the growing light. I followed it.

"Gradually, I began to hear tones coming either from a delicate instrument or a human voice. The tones were pure and sweet and unlike any I had ever heard. We had learned how to heal with color and tone, but these tones were beyond anything I had experienced. The light also began to change. What was once a pearl white light resembling moonshine, now began to take on other colors as well. Eventually, all the colors of the spectrum, as well as some that I had not seen, began to dance and twirl through the beams of light that I was following. The light and tone was familiar to me in some way. It reminded me of something that I knew just beyond the conscious reaches of my mind. As I became absorbed in the light and sound, my fear faded and was replaced with a stillness and peace that I had not known since I had entered the caves. The bleeding stopped and my wounds, both physical and mental, began to heal. My heart became light and joyous, and my mind clear of doubt and guilt. I fell to the ground and thanked the Goddess.

"'Oh, Beloved Mother, if I am to die now, I thank you for allowing me to do so in this way. I am at last at peace and I surrender my body, heart, mind, and spirit to you. In deepest love and gratitude, I give my life to you.'

"Then I saw her. It was the Goddess Athena. She stepped out from behind a final turn in my path and stood before me in complete Love and Majesty.

"'Arise, my dear. My Priestesses do not kneel upon the ground, but rather, stand tall in complete dignity and power.'

"Your Priestesses? I questioned in my mind. What could she mean?

"'If I have chosen you to be a representative of the Goddess, do you defy me by allowing doubt and insecurity to enter your heart?'

"'Oh no, Goddess. I do not doubt you. I surrender my life to the service of you and the Truth that you represent. Of all the Goddesses to whom I have called, you have always touched my heart the most. I have had many dreams of meeting you and given many offerings to your sanctuary. To be your representative would be the greatest of all honor.'

"'Would it be more important than having a husband, children, and a life outside of the temple?'

"'Yes, yes!' I spoke without a shred of doubt or confusion. 'Now, a life of servitude to a husband and a family seemed unimportant when I could be of service to the Goddess. I lovingly and completely accept this opportunity.'

"That is when the great Pallas Athena touched me. She took a wrap from behind the rock near which she stood. It was the color of moonbeams, and when it moved it reflected all the colors of the rainbow, and more. She came to me, and with her own hands, she draped it around my naked form and fastened it over my left shoulder with a silver pin shaped like an owl, the symbol of her wisdom. She then gave me this necklace that you see me wearing today. She carefully placed the amethyst upon my heart and told me to always wear it.

"My first thought was that I would damage this lovely garment in the murky water that I would have to cross to return. She smiled at me and said,

"'There is another way that is not filled with darkness and fear. Follow my light, Dear One, and the way shall open before you.'

"I tried to bow before her, but she would not allow it.

"'You are a representative of the Goddess; you bow before no one!'

"With these final words, Pallas Athena again stepped behind the bend. When I looked after her, she was gone. However, her light was before me as well as her voice. I don't know how long it took me to return, but the entire time that I followed her light, I heard her voice. She told me many Mysteries that I cannot share with anyone, even you, a component of myself. When I was at last free of the maze, I found myself at the cavern where the Oracles gave their readings to the many who sought counsel.

"In the center of the cavern was a large opening into the Heart of the Mother, Lady Gaia. No one knew how deep this orifice was. If one were to drop a rock into it, they would not hear it land upon the bottom. Sometimes a steam or vapor would rise from this opening, and sometimes it was very calm and still. There was a curved bridge which rose high above the orifice with a large chair placed over the very center of the opening to the Mother. The Priestesses would ascend a ladder on the east side at the time of the rising sun to get to the chair and descend the chair from a ladder on the west side at sunset.

"It was sacrilege to climb the curved ladder and to sit upon the golden chair of the Oracle without permission of the High Priestess. I did not care. The great Athena's voice had instructed me to do so, and I would hear her voice above all external ones. I do not know how long I sat upon the chair, as time or space did not limit my body. I traveled the inner galaxies and learned many lessons. When the High Priestess found me, she knew by my Light and attire that I had permission from sources higher than her own. I had passed the initiation that I was unaware I was taking, and I was a full-fledged Oracle for Delphi.

* * *

Shature was suddenly aware that she was sitting across from Matia and was again in the circular patio. She had become so enmeshed in Matia's story that she had become it. She had sat upon the Throne of the Oracle and had heard the Mother's voice as it spoke inside her heart.

"You were able to merge with my story and live that life as I recounted it," remarked Matia.

"But what of the decision that you were to make in your twenty-fifth year?" asked Shature.

"Yes, the decision. If you are ready, we will return to OUR story."

"Please," Shature eagerly replied.

Matia stood, and Shature instinctively followed her lead. Matia walked around the circular pool and stood directly in front of her.

"Let us merge into one being before we continue," spoke Matia.

Shature and Matia lifted their hands to the level of their hearts and joined them, palm to palm. Slowly, they could feel themselves merging. Shature felt the copper bracelets cool upon her upper arms and the weight of the amethyst necklace heavy upon her breast. She felt the soft gossamer gown that had been given to her by Pallas Athena and the silver owl that held it in place. Her hair was pilled high on her head and, as the soft ocean breeze played with her hair; the wispy curls tickled her cheeks and the nape of her neck. On her feet, she wore simple sandals and she was standing upon the fertile soil of Earth.

Shature and Matia together sent roots down from their feet deep into the body of the Mother. These roots, carrying their consciousness with them, traveled deeper and deeper, past the topsoil, into the sand, past the bedrock, and into the caves where Matia had received her enlightenment. Yes, the Goddess was alive here, pregnant with all life.

Deeper still they traveled. Down, down into the molten core of the Earth, where they surrendered their spirit flame into that of the Mother's. Now, their flames were one with Mother Earth's flame. Light as a feather, they floated again to the surface where their combined essences re-entered their forms. Shature had completely merged with Matia now, and, in so doing, she had merged with the Mother.

From deep inside her expanded being, Shature could feel her legs pull nourishment from the earth. She felt the sweet love of the Goddess travel up her body. From her solar plexus, she communed with the waters of Her great oceans and all the life that lived within them. She remembered how Her creatures had first crawled from these waters to learn to live upon the land and in the air. She could hear the call of each life as it spoke to Her of its needs, knew of the growing of each plant, and felt the weight of every mountain and hill. Within Her heart was Unconditional Love for all that lived upon Her. Like a mother, she felt the birth of each babe and the opening of each flower. Her emotions changed the weather and the sky echoed Her thoughts. She witnessed the continuous rising and setting of the Sun and felt the pull of the Moon as it circled Her.

Then Shature's awareness expanded to encompass the entire solar system where she welcomed an energy field of love radiating from Father/Mother Sun keeping each brother and sister planet in orbit. Venus sent a special ray of love to her dear sister, Earth. This love further expanded her consciousness, and she became a traveler in the Milky Way. The Great Central Sun beckoned her Home. The Milky Way now encircled her and she was a body of life within the vast expanse of space. Off in the distance, at the very edge of Her Universe, she saw a star. It was Father/Mother Sun and it was calling her -- calling her home to Earth.

With a gentle tug, she traveled instantly back to the Sun, back to Venus, and back into a small body that was preparing to journey . . . back to Earth. The jolt was so intense that Shature's eyes flew open. She saw Matia before her and, deep in Matia's violet eyes, she saw herself.

CHAPTER ELEVEN

IN SERVICE TO THE GODDESS

Without a word, the two women with joined essences sat down upon the circular bench facing each other. They could see both the pool and the Ocean of Light from the edges of their vision. Shature, though thoroughly grounded in her Venusian body, could still feel the Heart of Mother Earth beating in her chest. She felt the pull of the solar system about her and could see the Milky Way from the perspective of the Great Central Sun. Shature simultaneously experienced Earth's third dimensional Universe and fifth dimensional Venus. Her consciousness had expanded, and she could now hold more than one dimension at a time in her awareness.

Matia, firmly holding Shature's hands, resumed her story.

* * *

"For many years, I served as an Oracle. We only sat as Oracles from the new Moon until the last day of the full Moon. Then, as the Moon began to wane into her darkness, we stood down from the chair and spent our days in self-reflection and service to others. The men who came to us wished us to serve them at all times, but we refused. We still held our power, as we were Priestesses and they could NOT make us do what we did not want to. We were one of the last bastions of female power, and we knew it. We held a heavy responsibility for all of womankind.

"We would determine which of us would sit upon the chair by divining how each person's biorhythm was synchronized with the Mother's. We would check our star chart, use the pendulum, read the cards, or other methods. Zulia and I remained fast friends. We were no longer attached like children, but we were often together in our relaxing time and would help to determine each other's biorhythm. Zulia was especially expert at reading the cards, whereas I was expert at the star charts. The doubt that had so plagued me in my early youth was gone from me. I felt completely fulfilled and at peace with my destiny. Then, one day, something happened.

"Earlier that day when Zulia was reading my cards, she casually asked me if I was on the verge of a major decision. Suddenly, for the first time, I remembered the prophecy of my childhood. I also realized that I was just a few days from my twenty-fifth birthday. A deep terror struck my heart. The terror seemed so inappropriate to the situation that I said something inconsequential, abruptly fled the room and ran through the caves to the hidden valley. Each of the senior Priestesses had a certain area, which they had chosen to be just theirs, where they could find solitude and garden their herbs and flowers. When, at last, I was within the valley, I went to my special place to settle down and calm my heart and mind.

"How could I have forgotten that I was to have a special challenge at this time, and why was I so terrified by it? I had mastered many portions of myself. How could I have left such a gap in my self awareness? I tried to go inside, but my emotions were so strong that they closed the doorway to my heart. I found to which working with the earth and plants of the Mother grounded me and allowed me to communicate more easily with the Goddess, so I picked up my small shovel and spade which I kept there. I took to my gardening with a passion, breaking off dead flowers and leaves, pulling unwanted plants, and harvesting and nurturing certain herbs or flowers that needed it. Before I knew it, the sun had moved significantly across the sky. Had I managed to hide from this issue again?

"'No, my dear,' came a sweet and clear voice that I knew at once as the Goddess Pallas Athena. 'You will not be able to hide from this challenge. You must not judge yourself or your decision. Plans were made at higher levels that you have already consented. Listen with your heart now, and the way will be revealed to you.'

"Then my Beloved Athena enveloped me in her essence and took me to those higher places that she had mentioned. When I returned to the physical world, the Sun was low in the sky. I did not remember all of where I had been, but I felt calm and confident. I still did not know what my challenge would be, or the decision I would make regarding it. However, I had dedicated my life to the service of the Goddess and I would allow Her to show me my path.

"It was time to return to my everyday life and await my destiny. Night came quickly in our hidden valley, as it was completely surrounded by high mountains, but I was covered by dirt from my gardening. I changed my return route in order to cleanse myself in the clear pond at the South end of the valley. This part of the valley was off the regular pathway and was seldom used by anyone, as there were water supplies available to us at more convenient places. Also, I had greatly enjoyed my solitude and was still not quite ready to meet any of my Sisters.

"I arrived at my isolated bathing spot, removed my soiled garment and entered the pond. The water was pure and gentle against my skin, and I took a long, luxuriant bath. Finally, I arose from the water. Just as I was wrapping my gown about me, I heard what sounded like a groan. I followed the sound and, much to my surprise, saw a MAN lying in a pool of blood. I was at the very end of the valley and immediately next to the steep cliffs that descended sharply into the valley. I could see in the fading light that the man had fallen from the heights of the mountain down into our secret valley. What was I to do? No man must know of this place. But I certainly could not kill him or leave him to die. I pulled the unconscious man to the edge of the water and bathed his wounds, using torn portions of my gown to wrap them. As if the Goddess had known, some of the herbs that I had harvested were the exact ones that I needed at that moment to treat him. Luckily, he did not awaken before I had a chance to cover his eyes with more portions of my garment. He must not become aware of our valley.

"I could only hope that he would not awaken before I could pull him into the cave. Maybe his injuries would be extreme enough for him to forget that he had fallen into our secret valley. We had been trained in moving ill and injured persons, as all of us were given at least some training in the arts of healing. I checked his body to see if his back or neck was injured. It appeared they were not among the many broken bones of his body. I would have to risk moving him. I could not leave him there because he was beginning to move in and out of consciousness. I wrapped the remains of my gown around his body like a sack, leaving free his arms. Putting my arms under his and across his torso, I dragged his unconscious body back to the cave.

"He awakened before I reached the entrance of the cave, but did not have the strength to remove his blindfold. I lied to him about covering his eyes and said it was because of a head wound, and he was too foggy to care. He had received a bad blow to his head, and by the looks of the dried blood on his body, he had been on the valley floor for many hours. I could only hope that he would not remember what he had seen.

"Great excitement ensued when I dragged an injured man into the cave from the hidden valley. I was so exhausted that I practically dropped him as soon as I pulled him around the bend from the cave's entrance. Instantly, there were many of my Sisters there to assist in transporting him to our Healing Quarters. There were many healers more qualified than I to care for him now. So why could I not forget him? Why did I find myself following them into the healing area, taking only a short moment to grab a new garment? The healers and I worked through the night to save the man. He had broken both legs and his left arm in three places. His head had been injured very badly. He was bleeding through his nose and tried to throw up even though his stomach was now completely empty. For three days we worked over the man. I was surprised to find that my healing skills had been under-emphasized. Perhaps this was the decision. Maybe I was to be a healer rather than an Oracle.

"Later, I realized that I had made a big mistake in staying with the man so long. There is a saying that if you save someone's life, they are beholden to you, but it happened the other way around for me. In becoming so involved in his healing, I created a disease in myself. Because Mikeal was a young, virile man, he healed amazingly quickly. He was the darling of the Healing Quarters, but, unfortunately, he had eyes only for me. I didn't know why he fell so deeply in love with me. He couldn't have known that I was the one who found him until someone told him. His love for me was something with which I did not know how to deal. I had made a decision long ago to dedicate my life to the service of the Mother and the Goddess Pallas Athena. But the love that came from Mikeal's heart was causing me to again doubt my decision. I spent countless hours in front of Pallas Athena's altar in contemplation. However, she did not speak to me. I had analyzed and gone over her few words in the valley many times. I tried repeatedly to return to the place that she had taken me, but I was too disturbed and confused.

"I realized that with every day I was thinking more and more of Mikeal. I began avoiding him, which only caused him to get on his crutches quicker in order to find me. If he had acted like a whipped puppy, I could have gotten over him. However, even balancing on crutches and pursuing me through the caverns inside our cave, he remained dignified and masculine. Finally, one day, he said that he would seek me out no more. If I wanted to see him, I knew where to find him. My heart was breaking as he hobbled away from me, perhaps forever. I wanted to run after him and follow him to the ends of the Earth. But I was strong. Or was I? My work began to suffer. My readings upon the chair became confusing and obscure and my other duties were carried out in a half hearted manner. At last, the High Priestess called me for a private consultation.

"'My dear Matia, do you think that a community of Oracles cannot see what is happening to you?'

"I looked at her with an ignorance that only one who is lying to themselves can display.

"'Beloved Goddess! Do you not even know what is wrong with you?'

"I shook my head, hoping that the movement would not force my pent up tears to fall upon my face.

"'My Dear,' she spoke, as she gently reached over to touch my hand. 'You are in love with Mikeal.'

"Hearing the truth that I had kept from myself for so long released the dam of pent up tears. I fell to my knees before the High Priestess sobbing. She allowed me to place my head into her lap and gently stroked my hair while I cried out my pain and confusion.

"Finally, when I could cry no more, I arose again to sit before her.

"'What am I to do?' was all that I could say.

"'Well, I only know that you are no good to us in this condition. Take some time to sort things out in your heart. Remember that the decision you make is one you will have to live with for a very long time, perhaps, for the rest of your life.'

"I nodded and kissed the High Priestess' Ring of Authority.

"'Go now. I will speak with you when you have had some time to ponder your situation. Call to the Goddess, my dear. She knows much of love and will assist you if you allow it.'

"When I left the High Priestess, I knew that I had to talk to Mikeal. I went to my Sleeping Quarters to refresh myself and change my gown. I found Mikeal, not in the Healing Quarters, but in the sunny fields behind them playing with a dog. He looked over at me as the small dog ran after the stick he had thrown. There was no surprise in his face. He knew that I would come to him!

"'This is my dog. He led me to your valley and to you.'

"I rushed to his side to silence him.

"'Please, do not say that. We found you at the edge of the cliffs near our cave.'

"'Why does everyone tell me that? I have said nothing, as I believe that a lie shared by so many must have a reason. I did not want to get you in trouble. Were you not supposed to be in that valley?'

"'Why do you think that you were in a valley?' I hoped that I could still convince him of our lie.

"'Dearest Matia, I remember the fall. My dog, who has found me again, had run after a small animal and had become trapped on a ledge near the top of the mountain. The climb was steep, but I was in good health, and I set out to rescue him. After I saved him from his predicament, I found that I was in one of my own. There was no way to go down from there so I had to go farther and farther up the cliff in order to return to the base of it. When I finally reached the top of the cliff, I found a beautiful valley on the other side. Unfortunately, I was so enamored with the view that I did not notice the loose shale beneath my feet.

"'The drop was straight down. I did not know if the yell I heard in my ears was my dog or I. I hit the side of the hill several times before I finally passed out. At last, I awoke to find that the morning sun was now high in the sky and that I could not move. I could see the small pond close by, but was only able to drag myself with my one remaining uninjured limb to the shade of the bush under which you found me. I lay there, moving in and out of this world until you came to my rescue.

I was not surprised to look into your eyes as you leaned over me. I had been waiting for you the entire day.'

"'What can you mean? I did not know that you were there until the moment that I found you,' I replied, forgetting to continue the lie that my sisters and I had agreed on.

"Mikeal balanced himself on his crutches and, taking his one good arm, held my face in his powerful hand. Looking deep into my eyes, he said, 'As I lay there on the edge of death, I heard your voice. I am coming. I am coming. You called to me over and over. What a sweet and pure voice, I mused, in my foggy mind and open heart. Only the Goddess herself could speak with such a voice. And then when you found me, you comforted me with that same voice. I did not know if I was in the Other World or this one, but it did not matter. I had found my Beloved.'

"'No, No!' I cried, 'It was the voice of the Goddess Pallas Athena. She had called me also. It was she who you heard -- not me. She brought me to that pond. She is the one you must love. I am not free. I am a Priestess. I am not to have a man in my life. I have dedicated myself totally to the Goddess.'

"I realized that I was on the verge of hysteria. He put his strong arm around me and pulled me to his side. I leaned on him as he leaned on me.

"'Perhaps it was the Goddess who called me,' he whispered in my ear, 'but it was your voice I heard!'

"We walked, leaning against each other, to a small sheltered area underneath a huge tree which I had used many times to find solitude. We leaned against the tree together and gradually slipped down the trunk to the moist soil beneath it. We embraced each other in a love and passion that I had not known until that moment. Every thought left my mind. I don't know how we made love with all of his wounds, but we did. And it was divine. I felt the Goddess within my Soul in a way that I never had before. And he was a God. Our auras blended into one, and, at the climax of our love-making, we journeyed off into the Higher Worlds together.

"We awoke with the ground beneath us damp and cold. The Sun had fallen below the horizon. My Sisters would miss me yet they would know what I had done. The decision that I had been unable to make in my mind was made in my heart. The next morning I went to the High Priestess and told her of my decision. Mikeal would be able to travel within another moon cycle.

I would take the time to train others to take my place.

"The next moon cycle was the most difficult time of my entire life. I was trapped between two worlds. I was not of his world, but I no longer fit in my own. I had told him that he must not share his story with anyone. I told him that the penalty for a man knowing of our valley was death, and that we would both die if they found out that he remembered. I made him swear that he would tell no one. He promised me that he would do nothing to endanger me or endanger that which I held so close to my Soul. I tried to tell myself that I was leaving with him to protect the secret of the valley. But deep down inside, I knew that I was really going with him because I loved him. And soon enough, I knew that I had to leave because I was with child. The passion of our first lovemaking was so strong that an awaiting soul could not miss the opportunity to enter a body created by such love.

"I went about my work as usual. Mikeal and I met only occasionally. For me to be with a man while I was a Priestess would be sacrilege. We did not touch again with our bodies, but our souls were intertwined. I began to hear him talking to me telepathically, and he said that he also heard me. How could a man have such powers?

"Zulia did not speak to me for two weeks, and I realized that I was avoiding her as well. How could I make her understand my feelings? I would not endanger her by telling her that Mikeal remembered the valley. Finally, she found me alone deep in the cave gathering the stored herbs to bring to the Healing Quarters. I could no longer be an Oracle, as my own thinking was too cloudy. Instead, I continued the expansion of my healing knowledge. Perhaps my inner self knew that I would have need for it in my new life. It appeared that our meeting was accidental, as Zulia seemed as surprised as I did. She turned to walk away, but I caught her arm and she turned on me like an angry mother cat.

"'How can you do this?' she cried, with tears in her eyes.

"I found that I had no answer to her question. I didn't know how I could leave or even why I had to, except, of course, for the baby. But even that was not the reason. We knew how to terminate an unwanted pregnancy.

"'I only know that I must. I cannot answer your question because I cannot answer my own. There is just something in my heart that is leading me.'

"'I think that the guidance is not coming from your heart!' she retorted, with venom in her words.

"'I know that I have hurt you and abandoned you in a most cruel way. I don't expect that you will ever forgive me, nor will I forgive myself.'

"My words softened her, and she embraced me as we had done since we were children.

"Sobbing in each others arms, she said, 'Dear Matia, I understand more than you may know. I, too, have known love, but have not yet consecrated it.'

"'Zulia, my Sister, when did this happen? I have been so absorbed with myself that I have not been your friend. Have you found it to be as challenging as I have?'

"'I don't know if he loves me in return. His name is Zoran. He works outside our cave assisting the ones who come to the Oracle. Our eyes have met for many months, but I have kept my heart in the lap of the Goddess. But now that you are leaving to follow your love, I am faced with a doubt that I was able to control before. I am sorry that I have neglected you in this time of your need. I, too, have become absorbed in my own problems.'

"I smiled and kissed her warmly. 'Dear Zulia, we are doing the same thing at the same time, again!'

"We hugged, laughed and talked like girls for hours. What would the High Priestess have thought if she could have seen us? Zulia did not know if she would leave with her man, as she did not even know if he would ask her. But our love was renewed. As we returned to our comradeship, I realized how much I had missed it in the last few weeks. How could I live the rest of my life without seeing her? That was when the sadness overtook me. Perhaps I had made the wrong decision. Perhaps I should stay in the life that I had so loved, rather than venturing out into the unknown.

"Zulia gave me my answer. She was leaving. Zoran had indeed loved her also and could no longer stay away from her. However, they were not as lucky as Mikeal and me. They were found in the act of making love in a Sacred Grove. Zulia was expelled from Delphi. At her hearing, I stood next to her and told them all that I, too, had been with a man. We were both expelled from the Order. Others made my decision, and I did not have to carry the guilt of it. I was angry now, not for myself, but for Zulia. How could they have treated her so unjustly? Why was being with a man such an evil act? Did the Goddess not mate with men? Why then couldn't her Priestesses? All the teachings that I had learned in the innocence of childhood were lost in the passion of adulthood. Zulia and I left on the same day. I was never to see her again.

"I will now move the story of my life forward twenty-one years to this very patio. My life with Mikeal was beautiful. We had disagreements, of course, the main one being my constant need to remind him of my power. He had not chosen a traditional woman to be his wife. He had chosen a Priestess, and I would not give up my power as easily as I had given up my body. Although I had to put on a certain degree of an act for those around us in order to protect his image as a 'man', secretly, we were equals. All of our decisions were made together, except for one.

"It was a clear and warm day. We sat on this patio, as we had often done, having a slow, relaxing meal. We looked out across the ocean, as we had a thousand times, but the contentment that it usually gave me was gone. Life had changed much in the years since I had left Delphi. Now men were allowed to study the way of the Goddess and freely walked the secret valley with the women. I thought often of Delphi. I missed it more and more with each passing day. Perhaps it was because I had lived the life of a mother and wife for many years. I had borne ten children, and seven of them had lived. My last child was a daughter Zulia, and she was now seven years old. I had named her that because my beloved Sister Zulia had died just before my final pregnancy. Zoran had mortified her by taking a concubine, and Zulia had thrown herself off a cliff. I had seen it all in a dream, but it was not verified for almost a year. Zoran had tried to cover up his grief, but in the end, the guilt was too much for him and he, too, ended his life by taking poison.

"The birth of my last child had almost killed me, or perhaps it was the knowledge of Zulia's death that had done the deed. But I had not been totally well for the last seven years. I had become somewhat of a local healer since I began my new life with my husband, and I used my knowledge and experience upon myself. However, within the last year, my health had taken a turn for the worse. I could still attend to most of my duties, and Mikeal and I still had a loving sexual relationship, but something was missing in my life. It took me much contemplation to realize that what was missing was Delphi. But how could I tell this to Mikeal? Thanks be to the Goddess, he was the one who told me. We had just finished our meal and the servants had cleared the table. We were having wine and watching the sunset. It was as glorious as ever.

"'Even the Sun leaves the sky, as I fear, my Beloved, you must leave me.'

"I was shocked at his perception of my truth. I shouldn't have been. He knew me as well as I knew myself. I turned to him with fear and hope in my eyes. Would he understand?

"'Of course, I understand you,' he answered my thoughts. 'You miss Delphi. Since Zulia's death you have not been the same, and your health has become increasingly poor. I fear that if I don't lose you to the Goddess, I will lose you to death.'

"I ran to him, and sitting on the ground before him, I threw my head into his lap.

"'Oh, my love, could you love me so much as to release me to my destiny?'

"'My dear, I have already lost you. Now, I can either be loving or selfish. I choose now to return to you what you have always given to me-- unconditional love. Perhaps in Delphi your health will recover. I read the letter that they sent you inviting your return. Please do not scorn me for invading your privacy, but I needed to know if they would take you before I released you. I have protected you for twenty-one years and I could not allow you to be disappointed. I was the one who first communicated with them, asking if they would allow their Priestesses to return now that they had changed so many rules. My only question is, what will be done with our daughter Zulia?'

"'I will take her with me,' I said, hoping that I had not disclosed that I had also been thinking of returning. 'Dear Mikeal, they allow men now. You can come with us.'

"'No, dear. That is your life. I have mine here. I will, however, visit you as often as possible. I thank the Goddess for my many years with you. I must stay here to direct our older children and carry on the life that we have created.'

"I know now that he was very concerned for my health. He was right, as usual. I died on my return trip to Delphi. As we climbed the final hill and I saw my beloved cave below, I realized that my life was leaving me. I pulled Zulia to my side. She looked at me with terror in her eyes.

"'It is too late for me, my dearest daughter. I thought that I was bringing myself to this wonderful place, but it is you that the Goddess has called.'

"Zulia put her arms around my neck and sobbed, 'No, No, Mother. You cannot leave me. I need you to help me.'

"'The Goddess is your mother, dear. She will help you now.'

"With these final words, my Spirit left my body. Below me, I saw my daughter crying over my empty form. I also saw the Goddess behind her.

"Pallas Athena met with me in Her ethereal body.

"'Thank you for bringing us our next High Priestess,' she said, as she escorted me HOME!"

* * *

At this point in her storytelling Matia paused, and Shature returned her focus from Delphi back to the cliffs of Venus. Matia released Shature's hands and gently touched her face as she spoke into her eyes.

"In the time continuum which you will re-enter, you will have a husband, children, home and a career. A gift that I would like to give to you is an awareness that I did not have in my life as Matia. This gift is the knowledge that we can be Priestesses at the same time that we are wives and mothers. I did not acknowledged all the service I gave to the Goddess while I was married and raising children. Everyone in our community knew me as a healer, and people came from far and wide to receive healing of both the body and mind. For many years, I practiced all that I had learned in Delphi while I carried out the responsibilities of a home and a large family. My dying thought was that I could not have both worlds at once. That thought has left an impression upon your psyche. Erase that thought now and replaces it with the Truth: Spirit knows no limitation and the Love of the Mother embraces all life."

Shature impulsively put her arms around Matia. The two embraced so deeply that they became one being again. Like the patio that was an integration of ancient Greece and Venus, they were an integration of Matia and Shature. When at last they released their connection, Shature said,

"Is that how it will feel when I rejoin the consciousness of my third dimensional self?"

"Yes, except that I naturally resonate to the seventh dimension as I, too, was able to return to the Oversoul upon my death. I have "lowered" my vibration to answer your call. The portion of your self that you will re-enter resonates at a lower vibration than you do as Shature. Let us merge into one being again. This time, place your consciousness in my perspective so that you can experience merging with a lower vibration of your self."

They stood and face to face, heart to heart, allowing the energy between them to connect. They again raised their hands to the level of their hearts and jointed them palm-to-palm. Again, they felt the Goddess join them as they merged. The connection between their consciousnesses became complete and they were one being.

"Now," said Matia telepathically, "see Shature standing in front of you and feel yourself as me."

Shature did as she was instructed and saw her own face before her. She had not looked at her image since she had come to Venus. There was no sense of ego here, as one's form was unimportant. Beings changed forms, such as she had done from Shature to Lamerius to Shature. The features of one's form were considered much like clothing on the third dimension. One could change form at will or decide to be completely without it depending upon the experience they were having.

As Shature looked at herself from the perspective of Matia, she saw her many faces. She saw Lamerius, she saw herself in Faerie, and she saw how she had appeared when she first entered Atlantis from Venus. A moment of discomfort passed through her in that memory, but a calm warmth replaced it. The pain of that life was now a lesson, a lesson that she could appreciate. She then saw the face of the many other realities that she had reviewed.

There was Francesca, first an innocent maiden and then a loving wife and mother. She saw Illiana with her chin tight in courage and protectiveness for her loved ones. The gambler came next to her vision, and she felt a pull at her heart. She embraced that portion of herself and loved him unconditionally. He looked at her, first afraid and then a slow smile crossed his haggard face. No, he would not play that last card game. Instead, he decided to return to his in-laws' house to face the wrath of his father-in-law and to care for his children. He owned a ranch. Perhaps he could learn to work it.

The face before Shature then changed to the deserter, the Priestess of Set and all of those whom she had encountered in the darkness, in the caves of her own denial. She embraced all these portions of herself and infused them with the light of her fifth dimensional Self.

Then she saw the radiant faces of Rahotep, How-ta-shai and she—Shature. From her perspective as Matia, she began to remember, and feel, how every life she had reviewed was a chapter in the complete story of her Oversoul.

"Good," smiled Matia. "Allow me now to continue my story."

Matia and Shature merged again, and the thoughts of Matia directed their joint experience.

* * *

"As I turned to follow Pallas Athena, I took a moment to fix my gaze upon my youngest child, Zulia. Pallas Athena had said that she was to be the next High Priestess of Delphi. But now she was a seven year old child, and she was crying over my abandoned clay form. Wait, what was that misty presence I saw comforting her from the ethereal planes. Why it was my dear friend Zulia, but – N0--it was a higher portion my daughter. Then I understood my daughter was indeed the reincarnation of my friend Zulia. I had named her correctly. Now that I was free of the illusion of the physical plane, I remembered that when I was first pregnant, I had gone in my higher body to offer a new life for my friend.

"'She was a suicide and has much karma to pay," spoke the Council of Twelve. "If you take this Soul into your womb, you may damage your life force. You may even die.'

"'I don't care,' I said. 'I have had a long and beautiful life. If I must, I can sacrifice it so that Zulia may have another chance. Besides I am a healer. Perhaps I can heal us both.'

"Well, it looked as though I did heal her. She was a strong, young girl and seemed to have a high destiny, if she could remain true to herself. She would be without a mother from a very young age, such as I had been.

"I then turned to Pallas Athena, 'May I say good bye to my husband and family?'

"'Of course,' was her reply.

"In an instant, I was in Mikeal's and my home. It was the middle of the night, but my beloved husband was not asleep. He was sitting on top of our bed. He saw me instantly and ran to try to embrace my ethereal form.

"'I stayed awake this evening because I knew you would come to me. I knew today, even before the messenger came, that you had died. I banished him from our home before he could finish his message, as if sending him away could bring you back. I have let you down, beloved. Perhaps if I had given more attention to you and less to our estate, your health would not have grown so grave."

"He threw himself at my feet and begged my forgiveness. I laid my ethereal form down next to him so that I could wrap myself around him one more time. With my new body of light, I found I was completely flexible and could change my form at will. In fact, my shape molded to his instantly and then I remembered.

"'Why you are Lamire! You are my Divine Complement!'

"I expected surprise from him, but instead he calmly said,

"'Love of my life, I have always known that to be true. How will I exist now without you?'

"'Oh, but, my dear, you shall never be without me. I shall live forever in your heart. When your time has come to leave this plane, I will join you again."

"For a long moment I merged into his form, and the two of us were one again. Then I felt a pull on my consciousness, and I knew that I must leave. I drifted above him and left him sobbing on the floor of our room.

"He is strong' whispered Pallas Athena. 'He will recover. There is much left for him to do.'

"I went then to the beds of each of our other children and bade them good bye. Our two older sons were in the military far from home. Pallas Athena, in her grace, allowed me to visit them as well.

"'Will any of them remember that I said good bye?' I asked.

"'In time,' was her only reply.

"I then entered the Fields of Elysium, as was the belief of that ego. I spent much 'time' there studying my past life and my other incarnations, just as you have done. After I had finished my lessons and released all attachment to my life as Matia, I was able to return to the Oversoul to transmute my energies into a higher dimensional life-form. I will share with you part of my experience with the Oversoul. Join me fully in this experience, but realize that each personal ego that has released itself from the bounds of third dimensional limitation and separation may have a different perspective of this same occurrence.

"We have chosen to incarnate again and again for two reasons. One, we have volunteered to continue with physical incarnation until the time of the great change at the close of the Great Cycle, which is the time-space that you will re-enter. Two, each experience of incarnation brings a greater depth to the Oversoul.

"My life as Matia was one of the few lives in which I shared a long and happy physical incarnation with my Divine Complement. In that way, I was truly blessed. When I left the Elysium Fields in the fourth dimension to raise into my fifth dimensional vibration, Lamire, who was still incarnated as Mikeal, joined with me in his higher vibrational self. The feeling of being both male and female instantly brought our attention to Venus. We, too, experienced the Crystal City and the yellow Venusian sky with its streaks of pink and violet. The city stood before us as a shimmering spectrum of crystal rainbow. The colors and tones led us through the open door and down a long hall made of crystal pillars studded with the jewels of many planets and solar systems. At the end of the hallway was the vortex. In front of it stood Sanat Kumara, Earth's Planetary Logos and Pallas Athena, the representative of the Goddess. I saw the emanation from the many higher vibrations that encompassed their multidimensional consciousness. I bowed before them, but they motioned me to rise.

"'You, too, have a multidimensional consciousness that echoes many octaves above your current perspective. Worship is for those who seek to find outside themselves what is already theirs in the Oneness of all life.' They spoke telepathically as one being.

"'If you decide to enter this vortex, you will be reabsorbed into that Oneness. You are permitted no questions as all answers must be found inside yourself – inside the doorway to the One.'

"Their speech seemed like a riddle, but I recognized its content. I knew that only a leap of faith and complete surrender could allow my entry into the Vortex.

"'I understand,' I replied telepathically.

"'They stepped apart and created a pathway into the vortex. They, of course, already knew my answer.

I moved forward in the floating sensation that is common on fifth dimensional Venus. The vortex seemed to move towards me as I moved towards it."

CHAPTER TWELVE

LIFE AFTER BIRTH

Shature, who was now in complete unified consciousness with Matia, saw the vortex before her and remembered the other vortexes she had experienced. There was the vortex in fourth dimensional Faerie that led to either third dimensional Earth or fifth dimensional Venus. There was the vortex she had entered when she and Lamire were united as Lamerius and journeyed to Arcturus, and there was the vortex that Rahotep entered during his great initiation. In her expanded awareness, Shature now understood that instead of many vortexes, there was only one. The vortex was an inter-dimensional gateway which allowed those who entered it to raise or lower their vibratory rate.

"No," the voice within corrected her. "You do not raise or lower your vibration. In truth, you EXPAND your awareness to encompass more and more of your true multidimensional self. The vortex is beyond the limitations of time and space.

It serves as a pathway between dimensions through which the finger of the Oneness can extend itself into its individual components and back again into the Source. You will understand more as you allow yourself this experience."

Shature was ready. She felt a strong pull from the vortex as she simultaneously leapt into its core. Again, there was the rapid swirling around her. Faster and faster it spun, like a tunnel of circulating light. She became dizzy and disoriented. The many tones and colors that were alive in the vortex raised her vibration—octave by octave—until she felt as if she would burst. At the point which she could stand no more, the colors and tones permeated her form and transformed it into a vague human shape that was no more than a wisp of light.

The swirling sensation then became internalized and she felt a million swirling vortexes permeate her being. Each spun at an increasing rate, creating a tapestry woven of the many components of her Self. The spinning continued until the point of critical mass was reached and—in a burst of light—it stopped. She was in the void beyond the vortex.

For time beyond time, she remained in the void until a distant light began its journey towards her. Her Soul smiled as she recognized it as

Arcturus. With this recognition, the void became filled with millions of stars. She wished to again visit Arcturus, but as the stars came closer, they began to encircle her. Faster and faster, they moved until they blurred into another vortex, a vortex made of stars.

This vortex transformed into a tunnel with a stream of light flowing through it. Shature could see that this stream originated in a distant lake. Like a salmon following its instinct, she traveled against the flow of the liquid light. It drew her into it and she found a current in the very center of the stream that, if she surrendered to it, carried her up to the Source. She surrendered to this current and allowed it to fill her with its emanations. She, too, was a drop of liquid light seeking its Source. As the stream within a stream continued its upward journey, she could feel the waters of life simultaneously flowing downward into the lower dimensions to gather experience. Onward she traveled past lake after lake. She felt the consciousness of Rahotep, How-ta-shai, and Matia guiding her with their combined experience. Could she continue in their paths? Had she completed her initiations?

Almost in response to her question, the liquid light stopped. Slowly at first and then gradually gathering speed, she felt the current taking her back, back into the lower dimensions. The current rapidly carried her, but she felt no fear. Rahotep, How-ta-shai, and Matia were within her, comforting her, assuring her. Suddenly, the current emptied her in a large lake. Instinctively, Shature knew she was in the third dimension.

"About you is every third dimensional existence that you have had, are now having, or will have upon the planet Earth," she heard the united voice of the three. "Begin your journey here."

Abruptly, the lake disappeared, and Shature saw herself in a huge stadium filled with people.

"These people are all you in your myriad third dimensional Earth realities. Feel the life force of each of them. Imagine that the bottom of the stadium represents the ancient times, and the top of the stadium represents the dawning of the year, 2000 AD. From your omni-location of Oneness, you can choose any seat in the stadium to experience a particular reality. You may notice that, even though you are aware of all of these people, they are only aware of themselves and the life in which they are absorbed. You have achieved multi-dimensional consciousness, and they have not.

"But wait, is that Illiana and Francesca turning their awareness to your omni-present essence? And yes, the others that you have visited are also aware of you. As you have awakened, they, too, have begun to awake.

"Now, fill this stadium to the top with liquid light, and it again becomes a lake, but each reality stays within the confines of its own time-space coordinates. There is a large waterfall that empties into this lake. Go now, stand under it and feel its waters upon you. Allow yourself to surrender to the influence of the liquid rays of light and feel your frequency rising as you float up the waterfall, higher and higher until you see another lake of liquid light.

"Pull yourself into this lake. As you swim with the innumerable fish, imagine that they each represent a different fourth dimensional reality. The confines of time and space are not as rigid here, and each fish can move out of its initial location and communicate with the others around it.

"Some fish are beautiful and others look like sea dragons. Love each of them for the experience they offer you. If you wanted to, you could hold each fish and it would tell you the tale of its existence, but that would keep you in these waters for years and years of your Earth time. Instead, find the waterfall that feeds into this lake and allow its liquid light to raise your vibration.

"Ah yes, feel the familiarity of the fifth dimension. Is it not clear? As you pull yourself into this lake, you can see that is filled with thousands of crystals that hold the divine blueprint for the realities also existing on the third and fourth dimension. Some of these crystals float in the liquid light and others rest upon the lake floor. Since the fifth dimension exists in the eternal Now, their location does not represent their time nor space. The crystals that are floating represent the realities in which you are a space traveler, and the grounded ones represent the realities in which you are bound to one planet. Yes, there are many floating crystals. However, you must release this experience or you will not be able to continue your journey. Find your waterfall again and stand under its flow.

"As the waterfall raises your vibration to the sixth dimension, you feel less familiar with the experience. When you first ventured down from the Source, the glimmer of a group identity began to enter your consciousness and the Archetypes of the lower planes were born. Here, you live in group-consciousness, but you have a sense of yourself as with the inkling of individuality a component of your archetypal energy.

"Float into the center of the lake, but keep a thread of your individuality so that you will not lose your self awareness. From here, imagine your omni-directional perception as you live in the Oneness. You are a drop of water and you share your experience with every other drop. Feel the complete unity of All That Is. Now, gradually, allow the currents of the lake to carry you to the waterfall, up to the seventh dimension of your Oversoul.

"Yes, there is the waterfall. Feel its liquid light as it caresses the vague memory of the form you once held. As you allow yourself to raise in vibration, hold on to our voice so that you can translate your experience into the mind of Shature. Feel the vibratory rate of the seventh dimension, and allow it to enter your heart so that you may feel the message of your Oversoul.

"Tell us now of your experience."

"I find it difficult to remain conscious of my identity," Shature spoke to the three. "I am potential and totally without form. Even the sixth dimension feels individuated in comparison. Here I am 'not yet', but I know that 'I am'. Therefore, I am beyond any conception of structure or limitation. I am becoming. I am fire that has not yet been lit and rain that has not yet fallen. Even the light is a potential. I am in a huge caldron which is empty and simultaneously full—full of potential."

"This is as far as you can go now," spoke the three. "There is still more for you to accomplish upon the third dimension, and the visions beyond will await your return. Now that you have seen the path, you will be able to travel it when you are ready. We have traveled beyond this point and have chosen to return to await the reunion of the remaining members of our Oversoul as they ascend with the dear Lady Gaia and Her body, Earth.

Then the vision disappeared, and all that remained was the void. Since there was no time, no space, no thought, no feeling and no form, Shature could have been there for all eternity or simply the blink of an eye. All was Spirit—Pure Cosmic Force—until, gradually, a sound began to permeate the total silence of the void. It grew louder and louder and kindled a recognition of something yet unknown. The deep peace and total serenity of the void bade all formless potential to remain within it, but the sound circled the nothingness and embedded into it, creating a thin filament of light in the form of a circle. With the birth of this circle of light, other filaments of light slowly began to materialize from the total blackness of the void.

These light filaments surrounded the small circle, causing a small flame to fan itself into existence in the center of the circle. Although the flame's consciousness was dim, its innocence drew more filaments of light to manifest from the void. In its first conscious act, the small flame transformed its circle into a heart and, in a sudden burst of light, the heart and flame were embedded into the matrix of a form—a human form.

At each point where the network met, there was a tiny vortex. These vortexes slowly began to decrease their spin as the flame within the core connected to each of them. With each connection, the flame of life grew in its awareness and recognized that it was taking a form. With this recognition, the flame became a fire, and the fire became aware that it was the heart of a body of light.

Off in the distance the sound returned. It was a cry, the cry of an infant. Not one that had been born, but one that was crying to be born. The cry became a pull, and the pull became a sensation—a sensation of movement and of gradual materialization. The tiny vortexes of light that outlined the form spun slower and slower and pulled the light body to another vortex.

Whereas the first vortex had been one of expansion, this was a vortex of constriction. Tighter and tighter, denser and denser, the swirling tunnel forced the body of light to fill in the matrix with consciousness. When the restriction was almost intolerable there was a wishing sound and the tunnel disappeared. The darkness was filled with a million specs of light.

Stars, the Lightbody now perceived stars. The sound was coming from one of these stars, and that star pulled the Lightbody into its orb. The star was now a sun, which was encircled by nine planets and an asteroid belt. The second planet from the sun, which felt particularity like home, was somehow different. The consciousness had remembered it as a beautiful planet filled with life. Now it appeared to be an angry explosion of gas and mist. And the cry, it did not come from there. It came from the third planet. Yes, that planet had been known to the consciousness as Earth. The thought of Earth submerged the consciousness into an individuation known as Shature.

Shature blinked as if suddenly awakened. She expected to see herself sitting again on the patio with Matia, but her vision was instead filled with the distant view of Earth. She could see the continents and the blue of the many oceans. She saw its moon as it encircled the orb. From this perspective, Shature realized that, just as a network of light surrounded her, a network of light also surrounded the planet Earth. In fact, she could now see the entire solar system outlined by the light matrix.

The resonance of a certain area upon the third planet felt so harmonious with her essence that it pulled her towards it. It felt comfortable—like home. As she moved in that direction, she again heard the sound. Yes, it was a cry. She remembered now. It was this sound that had drawn her back from the void.

"It is the voice of embodiment," responded the three. "It is calling you now."

In a flash, Shature was sucked into a dark cramped space.

* * *

"Where am I? I don't know this place," thought a small portion of Shature's consciousness.

The small area was very dark and there were many unfamiliar sounds and sensations. There was a steady beating that was frightening—yet calming; and she appeared to be floating in a kind of fluid.

"I don't think I like it in here. It is dark and lonely," spoke the small voice.

Shature felt confined within a tiny, dense form with no freedom of movement. She had just experienced total freedom with space all about her and now she was trapped in a dark and foreign place. Who was this small voice? Was it another portion of herself? Was this another life?

"Where is everyone?" spoke the small voice. "Not that there would be room for them. The last I can remember, there were great beings all around me with wondrous and beautiful wings. They showed me how to fly and make my environment change. Now, no matter how hard I try, I cannot fly, and the environment is the same ugly red and black no matter what I do or think. No, I definitely do not like this place. I want to leave now. This is not where I want I to be. If only I could remember how I got here. If only my friends were here. They could tell my teacher, and me—yes, now I remember, my teacher. Where has she gone? She could tell me where I am. Beloved teacher, please come. Come and tell me where I am, and how I get out of this awful place."

Shature tried to answer the small voice, but it was not aware of her.

"Why doesn't she answer? She has always answered me," continued the voice, oblivious to Shature's reply. "How could she have forsaken me? What have I done wrong? This must be some awful punishment. What could I have done to deserve this? I always studied my lessons, and I lived as I was instructed. I practiced what I was taught, and I helped the Earthlings who called me.

"Oh no, not that. It couldn't be. Could this be ... could this be what I have feared? No! I am not ready to go there. There are still too many memories, too many bad feelings. I cannot go back yet. I was just becoming adept at flying and communicating with the Spiritual Hierarchy. No, I simply will not! There must be a way I can change this.

"Oh--what is happening now?" called the small voice in terror. Shature tried to communicate with the voice, but it could not hear her through her fear. The small place had grown smaller still, and the walls were pushing the dense form through a tiny hole.

"No, I simply will not fit. The hole is much too small. I will be suffocated. No, no! Oh, this is awful. I do not like this. My top is very uncomfortable, and it is getting darker and darker," complained the voice.

The beating sound could hardly be heard now, but there were many other noises. There was an unbearable cracking noise and a loud rumbling. There were also other noises that seemed to be coming from outside of the small space. The dense body was being pushed further into a small tunnel.

"Stop it. Stop it! I want out of here," cried the voice.

Finally the pushing and the noise stopped. Perhaps now Shature could figure out what was happening. The small voice had said something that had triggered a memory, and she had almost understood when all that commotion started. She had forgotten now, but it was something about Earthlings. Yes, that was it. There was a cry - a cry of...

Oh no, not again, more pushing and noises. Her top hurt. *Hurt*, she hasn't felt hurt since she was on...

"Stop, stop! I will not fit in there!"

It was the small voice again and it was angry.

"Who is pushing me? I am getting very angry. This is enough."

They were going into the tunnel, Shature and the small consciousness of the dense form. Somehow, they would have to fit. Shature had to find a way out. If only she could remember. There was something about Earth and a cry. Shature tried to remember, but something was wrong with her. Maybe it was because of the denseness and confinement of the small form that she had entered. Yes, she could vaguely remember this feeling, but where and when?

Oh no, more pushing. The dense form was being pushed even farther into the tiny tunnel. There seemed to be a light at the end of it and they seemed to be moving towards it. Finally, at least they would be out of the darkness. Where were they going? Shature tried again to call out to the consciousness of the small voice.

"Where am I going?" spoke the voice, almost in response to Shature's call. "I am frightened by this change. I definitely do not like it in here, but at least it seems safe. I have no idea what awaits me out there."

Shature did not know how to make the consciousness hear her, but she could still love it. In her heart, she embraced it with unconditional love and understanding. Then Shature knew.

"The pushing is getting unbearable. If I don't get out of here soon I will die," cried the voice. "Dying, perhaps that's what I am doing. But what is dying? I cannot remember, but I know that it has something to do with Earth. There is that word again. Why do I keep thinking about Earth? I was so glad to leave it. Could it be that I am going - -

"Oh no, now the pain is awful. Pain! I haven't felt that sensation for a very long time. Why am I feeling it now? I am tired. I can't remember feeling tired in a long, long time. And time-- I can barely remember time. What is happening to me? I seem to be going backwards. All the things that I have worked so hard to learn I am now forgetting and all the things I had once forgotten, I am now remembering. Well, at least the light is getting very close. I am beginning to feel something on my top. Oh no, it is touching my top. Oh! It hurts! Stop it! Why does it hurt to be touched? I have only known touching as becoming one. Now there is something hard and dense touching me. I feel hard and dense. Oh, if I could only remember how to fly."

The small consciousness could not hear Shature, and it could not even feel her love. Shature felt helpless. She had become very attached to the small being and wanted very much to help it.

"Oh no, now I am being pulled and pushed at the same time," cried the voice again. "What do they think I am, a piece of meat? 'Meat' what is that? Why are these old words coming into my mind? I haven't thought of them since I was last on - - - OUCH!"

"Where am I now?"

Shature had not been able to communicate with the small being, but she could still experience everything as it did. They were in this very bright and noisy place with many dense beings moving about very slowly making strange sounds from their bodies. What was worse yet, was that a large dense male figure dressed all in white was holding them upside down by their feet.

"What is he doing?" questioned the consciousness of the newborn. She seemed to now be dimly aware of Shature's presence.

"I hope he isn't going to hit - - - OUCH! My, I made a sound, too."

The newborn now looked right at the misty form of Shature and said,

"I don't like this place, even more than the other place. Why did he hit me? I did nothing wrong."

Then the man in white put the crying infant into a cold metal thing and left her there while he attended to a woman on a table who appeared to be dead. A woman in white came and wrapped something around the baby's middle and poked her in the foot with something sharp.

"OUCH!" cried the infant consciousness. "This is awful. I want to go back to the dark place. At least it wasn't cold, and no one hurt me. Why will none of my teachers come? I am so lonely."

Then the consciousness seemed to focus directly on Shature.

"Please, please, help me. Tell me what just happened?"

"You were born," said Shature.

* * *

Shature tried to enter the body of the small whimpering form, as it lay abandoned on the cold, metal scale.

"Not yet," spoke the voice of the three. "The infant has been too traumatized by her difficult birth. Wait! Give her time to adjust to her small physical self and bond with her mother. Shature was concerned, but knew it was best to follow their advice. She would wait in the fourth dimension for the best "time" to enter the body.

However, the situation grew worse when she saw the infant's father. He was the very Soul who had been the father of the Priestess of Set. His body was different, but his aura and "feel" were the same. He did not appear to have learned his lessons in this life either.

"I must enter the infant's body soon," Shature told the three, "before the father repeats any of his prior misdeeds."

"It is true," they replied, "that he could do her harm. But if you enter before she is sufficiently grounded in the third dimension, you will do her even more harm."

Shature unwillingly retreated to the fourth dimension where she waited impatiently for an opportunity to enter the new life. She tried to make a connection with the infant, but all she achieved was to turn its focus away from the third dimension and into the fourth. Finally, when she observed the father's aura as he apparently "cared" for the baby, Shature could stand it no longer. She waited for the infants' nap time and entered her room. She saw the tiny human's consciousness float above the physical form. Shature moved towards it in the Lightbody form that she was wearing. The infant's night body rushed to her and instantly clung to her.

"I don't want to be in that body! I want to go with you to Faerie," the infant's consciousness communicated telepathically. My guides told me that there would be a better day and that I would live to see Angels and humans together, but I cannot wait. I do not like it here. Take me Home, Please!"

Then to Shature's shock she saw the physical form of the small human struggle for breath. Her tiny chest shook, shivered, and then did not rise at all. The baby's body grew stiff and rigid while her face began to turn blue. The life spark, which was to stay in the body even during the deepest sleep, began to slip out of the baby's forehead.

Shature tried to bring the infant's night body, which was grasping on to her, to the infant's physical form so that they could enter it together. However, the body was too immature and limited to accept Shature's heightened vibration. She could tell that the power serge of her vibration would literally short-circuit the small body.

"You must return to your body," Shature spoke as lovingly as she could to the infant's consciousness. She tried to mask her growing concern.

"No, I will not!" was the response. "I don't want that life. I don't want that father—again."

"Do you also recognize him?" spoke Shature.

"Yes, and I won't go back."

The baby was very much in danger of dying now. It lay totally limp in the crib and its face showed no expression, as it turned increasingly blue.

"Dear One," Shature called. "Help me." Then she remembered the Violet Fire. She surrounded the baby's body, herself, and the clinging consciousness in the Violet Fire. It did not seem to work. The life force of the baby still refused to enter the body.

Shature heard a click and saw a movement in the room. Yes, the door was opening. The baby's mother had come in to check on her. As soon as she entered the small room, she knew that something was wrong. She went over to the baby and tried to awaken her, but she didn't move. The now frightened mother picked up the baby in both arms and shook it trying to make her breathe. The baby did not respond.

"You must enter the baby," said Shature to the stubbornly clinging consciousness. "Your mother loves you and will care for you. She will leave the father soon and find you a new daddy—I promise."

"How do you know?" questioned the consciousness.

"Watch, time is different here than on Earth."

The infant consciousness watched as a scene was displayed before her. She saw a loving grandmother, grandfather and uncle with whom she was living. The father was gone, but he had visitation rights.

"No," the baby said to Shature. "He will still come and get me."

As the baby's consciousness was removing itself from the physical body, it was becoming more aware. Perhaps now Shature could reason with it.

"You have chosen this life yourself. In another reality, you could not say no to him until after your death. You chose him again as your father to give yourself a second chance to gain sovereignty as master of your destiny. I will show you a picture of what you can do in your future to heal your past."

Shature focused her mind and projected a hologram before them.

"I will show you this story from the mind of your future three year old self. Watch, and you will see how much power a small child can have."

* * *

It was such a sunny day, and the daddy had said he was going to take her to the pony rides and the train. However, he instead took his small daughter to the familiar dark room. The floor was wood and there was a round rug on the floor. The child liked sitting on it. Grandma and Mommy wanted her to sit in chairs, but she liked the floor better. It reminded her of something.

Then, suddenly, she saw herself sitting on a dirt floor. There was a fire in the middle of a round room. It was made of animal skins and everyone lived in it together. The mom and daddy slept under a fur and sometimes they did that thing. It sounded warm, sweet and happy. The feeling of Love was very strong, and it filled the round room like the warm, thick air.

NO---this room was not round. It was the rug, which was round, and it reminded the toddler of the plains and her spotted horse. In that picture, she was a boy. The toddler often had pictures fill her mind. Sometimes she became very confused as to which pictures were real and which pictures were her imagination. No, this room was not round. It was square with walls that went straight up with a roof on top. In the 'In-between', where she lived before she came here, they had houses sometimes, but those houses never had a roof. There, everyone wanted the Spirit to be able to fall upon them, even in an enclosed place. She looked up and saw the open sky above her.

No, she had done it again. She had moved into another picture. Maybe that was because she didn't really want to be where she was. She had discovered at a very young age that she could remember pictures in her head. If she really looked hard at them and tried to feel the picture, she would suddenly be there. However, it became too easy for her and sometimes she wasn't sure if she was in a picture or in the "real world."

But now, she was not riding a pony or flying with Fairies. She was with her Daddy. Her body was little and she looked very cute. She had twenty seven curls, just like Shirley Temple, and she wore a pretty blue suit and patent-leather Mary Jane's with her new white socks with ruffles. Her Daddy pulled up a short stool and placed it in the middle of the round rug right in front of the scratchy chair that was not orange and not brown. Daddy sat down in the chair and instructed his daughter to sit upon the stool. He wanted to play the game again. The toddler was afraid to ask about the ponies and the train ride. She was afraid because he was sending her that "feeling" that was NOT Love. She did not want to play the game. It was NOT fun. Why did he like to play that silly game? The child was looking down at her Mary Jane shoes and fiddling with the lace on her socks. Her Daddy told her to look at him.

Why did he want her to look? If he made her look, she would only look with her face and not her eyes. He didn't know that when he made her look, her eyes called "Him". Then, the pretty lights would come and she would watch a very pretty picture instead of her Daddy. But wait--what was that Love feeling? It was not coming from Daddy, but she could feel it. It felt just like when "He" came to her. Oh, and the lights were prettier than ever. Maybe there were Fairies in them?

The pretty lights, the dancing fairies and the feeling of love that she always got when "He" was with her made her feel like she had a big body. She looked around the room and saw Angels in every corner, all smiling and encouraging her to stand up for herself. But, he was a Daddy, and she was just a little girl.

"You are much more than just a child," spoke the kind female voice of Shature. "Remember who you are. You have great power."

This pretty lady that was always with her had told her many times to remember who she was. The child did not know what that meant except that whenever the lady told her that, she would see a whole bunch of new and wonderful pictures.

She looked at her Daddy again--this time with her eyes. He looked different now. He had a high hat and his face was hard and cold. He had a long black mustache that went past his chin and there were pretty rocks all over his hat. Suddenly, she was not a child. She was a woman. She knew this man and knew that he wanted to hurt her.

"NO! NO! NO!" her screams returned her to the small child's awareness. "You said we were going to the ponies and trains. I DON'T LIKE IT HERE! Who are you? You are NOT my Daddy! You are not nice and I don't want you for my Daddy!"

The child jumped up, knocking over the stool she had refused to sit upon and ran behind the fuzzy chair. She knocked over the tall lamp that had been the only light in the room. It fell to the floor with a crash. Now the room was very dark. The child did not stop screaming. The man stepped over the fallen lamp, reached behind the chair and grabbed the screaming child. She bit him and yelled with all her might,

"You are NOT my Daddy. You are NOT my Daddy. I don't want you for a Daddy."

The man became concerned that someone would hear the child and he tried to *shush* her, but she yelled even louder. He pushed aside the chair and grabbed the child. He held her high in the air and shook her to make her stop crying. The child became stiff and a fury covered her face. Time stopped.

"I will not die for you," she said in a woman's voice.

Shocked, the man looked into her face and was captured by her eyes. They seemed to be illuminated in the darkness of the room and they were staring right at him. No, right INTO him. Her eyes were not those of a child and held eons of experience. The light that shown from them filled the entire room and pierced his Soul.

Then he remembered. He could not hold the memory because the chill of it forced it from his mind. Even as it left him, he knew that he would not see his daughter again.

Almost gently, he placed her on the ground.

"I'll take you home now," he said simply.

* * *

With those final words, the scene disappeared and the crying of the terrified mother was the only sound that remained. Finally, in desperation, the mother had turned her baby upside down and shook her from her legs. The mother's love and determination as well as the consciousness' own new confidence in her self, pulled the wandering spirit back into its tiny body. With a loud cough, something that had been trapped in the baby's throat was dislodged and the baby took a deep breath. The mother turned the baby over and held her deeply to her heart while she sobbed into the crook of her daughter's neck. The baby's color came back as her full essence returned to the physical body.

Shature knew that she would have to wait longer. She, too, was convinced that the child would learn to take care of herself. Maybe then, she would be ready to envelope Shature's heightened vibration.

Shature would wait and watch over the child. Slowly, bit by bit, she could help her to remember. As she turned to extend herself back into the higher dimensions, she heard the small voice of the infant consciousness.

"Thank you for showing me how strong I would learn to be. Will you be there to help me more?"

"Yes," Shature replied with deep Unconditional Love.

"I shall always be there."

Epilogue

As the consciousness of Shature saw the final wisps of the infant's consciousness return to its body, she noticed that the light form she was wearing disappeared. She was now a speck of light, a center of aware consciousness. Her formless state seemed to pull her back into the vortex. However, the journey was now calm and peaceful. She seemed to travel through all time and space while memories of her third and fourth dimensional lives swirled about her.

Shature instinctively knew that some higher vibration of the Oneness was summoning her. She did not understand what was happening, but she had learned to trust the "feel" of the Oneness. Feelings of complete love surrounded and comforted her like a blanket of Light. She could feel her formless state became lighter and lighter as she raised her vibration.

Off in the distance, she saw a vortex open and a beautiful being stepped through. It was Lamire. Instantly, Shature was by his side and they merged again into one being.

"Beloved," spoke Lamire from within their joined form. "I have come to wait here with you.

I, too, have a body that I will enter when he can tolerate my vibration. We shall meet my love. We shall meet upon the third dimension!"

"Oh, Lamire, do you think we will be able to recognize each other?"

"If we can recognize our Selves, we shall be able to recognize each other."

RECOGNTION OF COMPLETION

The stream of light
fell upon her head.

She felt it illumine
her deepest secrets
and bring them to the surface
of her consciousness.

She was not pleased
to see some of them,
yet others filled her
with the glory of Truth.

She had always known
that there was more.
There had to be.

Just this life,
just this reality,
just this consciousness,
would not be worth it,
Would not be a possibility.

This knowledge set her apart.
She was different from the rest.

There was no reason for her
to believe as she did.

No one around her told her
about the things she knew.
But inside, yes, inside
there was always someone.

When she was a child,
he was her friend.
When she was a teenager,
he was a secret love.

When she was pregnant,
he was her unborn child.
And when she needed him,
he was her Guardian Angel.

Always, always he was there.
When she was alone,
he held her hand.

When she was afraid,
he protected her;
and when she was sad,

he comforted her.

When no one smiled at her humor,
he laughed.
When no one answered her question,
he replied.
And when no one understood,
he knew her.

What was this presence?
Only she could keep it away.
If she didn't believe,
he was gone.

Or, if she fell into
the depths of emotion,
she couldn't hear him.

But just as soon as she recovered,
as soon as she believed again
in herself,
he was back.

She could lean her head to the right
and rest upon his shoulder.
She could feel
his arms about her.

Sometimes, she could feel him
brush her forehead,
as if to release the pent-up thoughts
that were forever in her brain.
So who was he?

Was he just a figment of her imagination?
Or was he the only reality
and everything else was an illusion?

Was he in her,
next to her,
beside her?
Would he leave her?
Would he ever show his face?

Oh, please,
let him show his face.
Let him enter
into her very soul
and take her with him.

If he isn't real,
then neither is she.

RECONSTRUCTING REALITY

If he doesn't truly exist,
then there is no reason.
There is no love.

He must be real.
He is her life.
He is her Self.

He is the part of her Self
that she has not yet become.

He is her completion,
the Divine Complement of herself.
The thread which will mend the tear.
The salve that
will heal the wound.
The other half that
will make her whole.

But how could she accept him?
How could she ignore
that which she hears outside
and listen inside to his
quiet voice above all others?

How could she remember
that she is special?

She does deserve,
she is complete,
she is whole.

She must.
She simply must.
Yes.

Yes, she feels his arms
as they enter hers.

She feels his feet
as they stand within her feet,

Hears his heart
as it beats within her own,

Feels his breath
inside her mind.

They are complete.

They are ONE
Together in
LOVE!

RECONSTRUCTING REALITY

About the Author

Suzanne Lie Ph.D.

Suzanne Lie, Ph.D., has been a seeker since she was a child where her active "imagination" took her deep into her inner life. Suzanne first stepped onto her spiritual path in the mid-1970s when she met her first spiritual teacher. Since then, she has had many teachers and initiations.

Her life in the physical plane was quite "normal" as her spiritual work provided her with the confidence to continue her educational training to obtain a Ph.D. in Clinical Psychology. Her studies included personal psychotherapy and focused on alternative methods of psychotherapy, such as hypnotherapy and guided meditation, which gave her tools to help herself, as well as others.

In 1999, after two years of prompting from the Arcturians, she began sharing her insights on her website, www.multidimensions.com, where her full spiritual journey is described. "Coming out" of the spiritual closet was not easy, but fortunately, documenting her journey and talking to others all over the world with similar experiences allowed her to fully accept and embrace her true SELF.

Once she built a solid foundation of knowledge regarding the journey back to the multidimensional SELF, she began writing the two volumes of the book, ***Becoming ONE, People and Planet: A Manual for Personal and Planetary Transformation.***

She continues to regularly share her experiences and Arcturian teachings on her blog, **Awakening with Suzanne Lie**, and she wishes to help awakening ones come out of hiding and allow the glory of their highest expression of SELF into their everyday life.

Explorations into the incarnation and connection of twin flames and divine complements are detailed in her book, ***Visions from Venus***, and her book ***Reconstructing Reality*** describes the process of awakening to past or *parallel* lives and incarnations.

She is excited to share her latest 5-book series, ***Pleiadian Perspective on Ascension***, which details the entire process of an ascending planet designed to assist humanity with its current transition into a higher dimension.

Recognizing the need for comprehensive educational training and guidance in multidimensionality, she has recently developed **Multidimensional Leadership Training** programs, in conjunction with the Arcturians, designed to train new leaders that will bring forth expanded, synchronistic guidance, support, leadership, and governance in the societal shift.

All of her initiatives remind us that through seeking, communicating with, and integrating our true, multidimensional SELF into our physical life, we can greatly expand our consciousness and regain latent skills that will assist us in creating our new reality.

Suzanne is available for personal sessions and would love to connect with and assist those ready to explore multidimensionality and who feel drawn to the Arcturian teachings.

www.multidimensions.com

Other Books by the Author
www.multidimensions.com

The Journal — When Ordinary People Get Extraordinary Information
When Lisa finally arrived at her childhood home, her mother was gone. All that greeted her was her mother's journal, which she decided to read.

A New Home — Pleiadian Perspective on Ascension Book 1
How it All Began — It's April eleventh 2012, and the California sun was still below the horizon. After a long complex dream of being in someone else's house, I realized it was time for me to leave. I got up and went into my office to receive this transmission. I am ready for your transmission now.

Life on the Mothership — Pleiadian Perspective on Ascension Book 2
There were just the two of us in the ship. I had not been on the Ship very long when I had my first experience of the Mothership's Oversoul. I had been there long enough, however, to understand that the ship was a living, multidimensional being.

The Landing Party — Pleiadian Perspective on Ascension Book 3
Mytre and Mytria have "landed" within the consciousness of earthbound Jason and Sandy and are in the process of assisting them to awaken to their Higher Self. Jason and Sandy meet each other, fall in love and totally alter their lives to encompass their greater purpose, which includes unlocking the mystery of their multidimensional reality.

It Is the NOW — Pleiadian Perspective on Ascension Book 4
Featuring a possible reality in which both humans and Pleiadians, with the help of Mytrian and the Arcturian, could serve in unity to transcend a planet. It Is The NOW is a "science fiction" that presents a possible reality of "scientific fact." Join us on our inter-galactic and inter-dimensional travels that bring us back to creating a new home.

Through the Portal — Pleiadian Perspective on Ascension Book 5
Big changes are about to occur on planet Earth, and leadership training is needed for Sandy and Jason. But when they return to Earth, that which they thought they would change, changed them instead. Follow this amazing "final act" that is actually a new beginning.

Becoming ONE, People and Planet: A Manual for Personal and Planetary Transformation Volume One
   This series is a masterful blend of psychology, metaphysics, ecology, science, art, and spirituality. This book offers information, meditations, and exercises...

Becoming One, Becoming ONE, People and Planet: A Manual for Personal and Planetary Transformation Volume Two
   This series is a masterful blend of psychology, metaphysics, ecology, science, art, and spirituality. This book offers more information, meditations, and exercises...

Visions from Venus, A Multidimensional Love Story, Book 1
   This journey begins with Shature's descent into the third dimension, then to a new home in the fourth dimension, and ends with her return to the third dimension in search of her other half. Fact and fantasy intertwine...

Reconstructing Reality, Book 2 of Visions from Venus
   Most of us do not remember that we have volunteered to remember our multidimensional heritage and unite with our true SELF in the higher worlds. Remembering this unity would be difficult

indeed with the knowledge of only one lifetime...

Thirty Veils Of Illusion

When Illusion is removed, all that remains is Truth. This book should really be entitled, "My Thirty Veils of Illusion," as I'm sure that each person who journeys inside himself or herself would find their own thirty illusions, or more...

Journey Through the Arcturian Corridor — Part I

The Arcturian Corridor is a tunnel of light, which serves as an inter-dimensional portal between the physical realms and the higher worlds of the fifth dimension and beyond...

The Journey Continues: Arcturian Corridor — Part II

The Journey Continues: Arcturian Corridor — Part III

Preparing for the Return: Arcturian Corridor — Part IV

Seven Steps to Soul: A Poetic Journey of Spiritual Awakening

Seven Steps to Soul is a poetic and therapeutic journey of spiritual awakening. The seven sections of this book represent seven processes that align us with our Soul...

What Did You Learn?
Welcome to the Land of Inner Peace and Limitless Joy. Have you learned the secrets of creating the reality YOU desire? For, indeed, life is YOUR creation. As the illusions of our physical reality end, and we return to…

The Violet Temple
Join us as we calibrate our consciousness to activate our personal Merkaba, so that we can take a Journey to the Central Sun, Alycone, The Pleiades. Once there, we will meet Mytria, who will guide us through the Violet Temple…

A Child's Adventure In Faerie – For The Child Within Us All
Most of us do not turn within to ask for answers until we are forced to do so by feelings of failure or experiences of fear and pain in our outer world. Our inner life may hold pain and sorrow…

More books on their way, so please stay tuned to **www.multidimensions.com**

Printed in Great Britain
by Amazon